Critical Acclaim for *PC/Computing How Computers Work*

"As an enjoyable way to learn what makes your system tick, nothing comes close to *How Computers Work.* Browse through it for an entertaining and informative diversion, or work your way through from cover to cover for a thorough orientation. And when you're finished, don't hide it away on some remote shelf—leave it out on your coffee table where everyone can enjoy this beautiful book."

—Alfred Poor, *PC Magazine*

"A 'real' book, and quite a handsome one…The artwork, by Mr. Timothy Edward Downs, is striking and informative, and the text by Mr. White, executive editor of [*PC/Computing*], is very lucid."

—L.R. Shannon, *New York Times*

"…a magnificently seamless integration of text and graphics that makes the complicated physics of the personal computer seem as obvious as gravity.
When a book really pleases you—and this one does—there's a tendency to gush, so let's put it this way: I haven't seen any better explanations written (including my own) of how a PC works and why."

—Larry Blasko, *The Associated Press*

"If you're curious but fear computerese might get in the way, this book's the answer…it's an accessible, informative introduction that spreads everything out for logical inspection. To make everything even clearer, White introduces the explanatory diagrams with a few concise, lucid paragraphs of text. Readers will come away knowing not only what everything looks like but also what it does."

—Stephanie Zvirin, *Booklist*

PC Computing

HOW COMPUTERS WORK

INCLUDES INTERACTIVE CD-ROM

PC Computing

HOW COMPUTERS WORK

INCLUDES INTERACTIVE CD-ROM

RON WHITE

Illustrated by
TIMOTHY EDWARD DOWNS

Ziff-Davis Press
Emeryville, California

Editor	Melinda E. Levine
Project Coordinator	Ami Knox
Technical Reviewer	John Rizzo
Proofreader	Kayla Sussell
Cover Designers	Timothy Edward Downs and Carrie English
Book Designer	Carrie English
Principal Technical Illustrator	Timothy Edward Downs
Additional Technical Illustrators	Carrie English, Cherie Plumlee Computer Graphics & Illustration, and Michael Troller
Page Layout Artists	Carrie English and Bruce Lundquist
Digital Prepress Specialist	Joe Schneider
Word Processor	Cat Haglund
Indexer	David Heiret

This book was produced on a Macintosh Quadra 900 and a IIfx, with the following applications: Adobe Illustrator®, QuarkXPress®, Microsoft Word®, MacLink® *Plus*, Adobe Photoshop™, FrameMaker®, Aldus® FreeHand™, and Collage Plus™.

Ziff-Davis Press
5903 Christie Avenue
Emeryville, CA 94608
1-800-688-0448

ISBN 1-56276-250-8

Manufactured in the United States of America

10 9 8 7 6 5 4 3 2 1

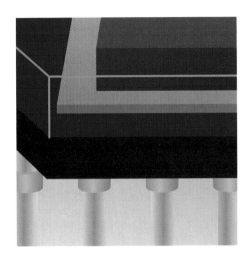

**For Shannon and Michael,
who always kept me honest
in my explanations**

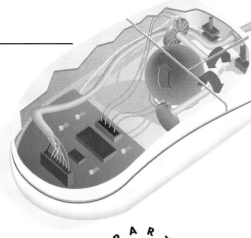

PART 4

Input/Output Devices

100

PART 5

Networks

150

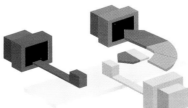

PART 6

Printers

166

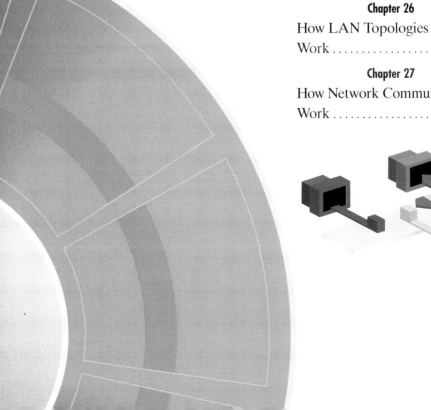
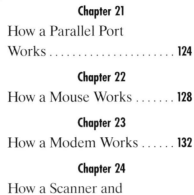

"How It Works" debuted in *PC/Computing* in 1989 as part of a new section of the magazine called "Help." It would be nice if I could say we instantly knew the best way to create illustrated explanations of how computer components and software work. We didn't. For a long time, I've wanted to redo some of our earlier efforts. This book is that opportunity, and it lets me rearrange into some sort of sensible order the often random selection of topics that appeared in *PC/Computing*.

I had the privilege of launching "How It Works," but over the years, many people have worked on it, and I'm grateful for the research and explanations they've done. Deep thanks go to Herb Brody, Brett L. Glass, Preston Gralla, Christine Grech, Marty Jerome, Raymond Jones, Matthew Lake, Jack Nimersheim, Randy Ross, Stephen Sagman, Jan Smith, Dylan Tweney, Doug van Kirk, Mark L. Van Name and Bill Catchings, and Kenan Woods.

I'm also grateful to the dozens of people in the PC industry who've shared their knowledge, schematics, and white papers to make *PC/Computing How Computers Work* accurate. And thanks to the many staff members at *PC/Computing* who helped me handle my job at the magazine while this project was going on; to former Publisher Mike Edelhart, who started the ball rolling on this book; and to Cindy Hudson and Melinda Levine at ZD Press, who were always tolerant of my cavalier disregard for such niceties as outlines and chapter numbers. And thanks to my wife, Sue, for her encouragement and her patience while waiting for me to pop out of writing mode.

I learned long ago that a writer's skill depends largely on how well the writer can borrow from others. In addition to the staffers and free-lancers who've contributed to "How It Works," three books were invaluable for details on PC innards: *Inside the IBM PC* by Peter Norton, *The PC Configuration Handbook* by John Woram, and *The Winn Rosch Hardware Bible* by Winn Rosch. Also helpful was *The Way Things Work* by David Macaulay, not only for its own informative explanations of computers, but for its examples of how to combine text and art into clear explanations.

Finally, this book would not be what it is without the artwork of Timothy Edward Downs. Invariably, Tim not only transformed my crude sketches into clear, informative illustrations, but also managed to make them into wonderful works of art. This book is as much his as mine.

Ron White
San Francisco

Any sufficiently advanced technology is indistinguishable from magic.

—Arthur C. Clarke

Sorcerers have their magic wands—powerful, potentially dangerous tools with a life of their own. Witches have their familiars—creatures disguised as household beasts that could, if they choose, wreak the witches' havoc. Mystics have their golems—beings built of wood and tin brought to life to do their masters' bidding.

We have our personal computers.

PCs, too, are powerful creations that often seem to have a life of their own. Usually they respond to a seemingly magic incantation typed at a C:> prompt or to a wave of a mouse by performing tasks we couldn't imagine doing ourselves without some sort of preternatural help. But even as computers successfully carry out our commands, it's often difficult to quell the feeling that there's some wizardry at work here.

And then there are the times when our PCs, like malevolent spirits, rebel and open the gates of chaos onto our neatly ordered columns of numbers, our carefully wrought sentences, and our beautifully crafted graphics. When that happens, we're often convinced that we are, indeed, playing with power not entirely under our control. We become sorcerer's apprentices, whose every attempt to right things leads to deeper trouble.

Whether our personal computers are faithful servants or imps, most of us soon realize there's much more going on inside those putty-colored boxes than we really understand. PCs are secretive. Open their tightly sealed cases and you're confronted with poker-faced components. Few give any clues as to what they're about. Most of them consist of sphinxlike microchips that offer no more information about themselves than some obscure code printed on their impenetrable surfaces. The maze of circuit tracings etched on the boards is fascinating, but meaningless, hieroglyphics. Some crucial parts, such as the hard drive and power supply, are sealed with printed omens about the dangers of peeking inside, omens that put to shame the warnings on a pharaoh's tomb.

This book is based on two ideas. One is that the magic we understand is safer and more powerful than the magic we don't. This is not a hands-on how-to book. Don't look for any instructions for taking a screwdriver to this part or the other. But perhaps your knowing more about what's going on inside all those stoic components makes them all a little less formidable when something does go awry. The second idea behind this book is that knowledge, in itself, is a worthwhile and enjoyable goal. This book is written to respond to your random musings about the goings-on inside that box that you sit in front of several hours a day. If this book puts your questions to rest—or raises new ones—it will have done its job.

At the same time, however, I'm trusting that knowing the secrets behind the magician's legerdemain won't spoil the show. This is a real danger. Mystery is often as compelling as knowledge. I'd hate to think that anything you read in this book takes away that sense of wonder you have when you manage to make your PC do some grand, new trick. I hope that, instead, this book makes you a more confident sorcerer.

BEFORE YOU BEGIN

This book has been written with a certain type of personal computer in mind—the IBM PC-compatible computer, usually powered by an Intel microprocessor and most often running the MS-DOS operating system. Many of the specifics in these explanations apply only to that class of computer and those components.

In more general terms, the explanations also may apply to Macintosh computers, Unix workstations, and even minicomputers and mainframes. But I've made no attempt to devise universal explanations of how computers work. To do so would, of necessity, detract from the understanding that comes from inspecting specific components.

Even so, there is so much variety even within the IBM/Intel/MS-DOS world of PCs that, at times, I've had to limit my explanations to particular instances or stretch the boundaries of a particular situation to make an explanation as generic as possible. If you spot anything that doesn't seem quite right in this book, I pray that my liberties with the particulars is the only cause.

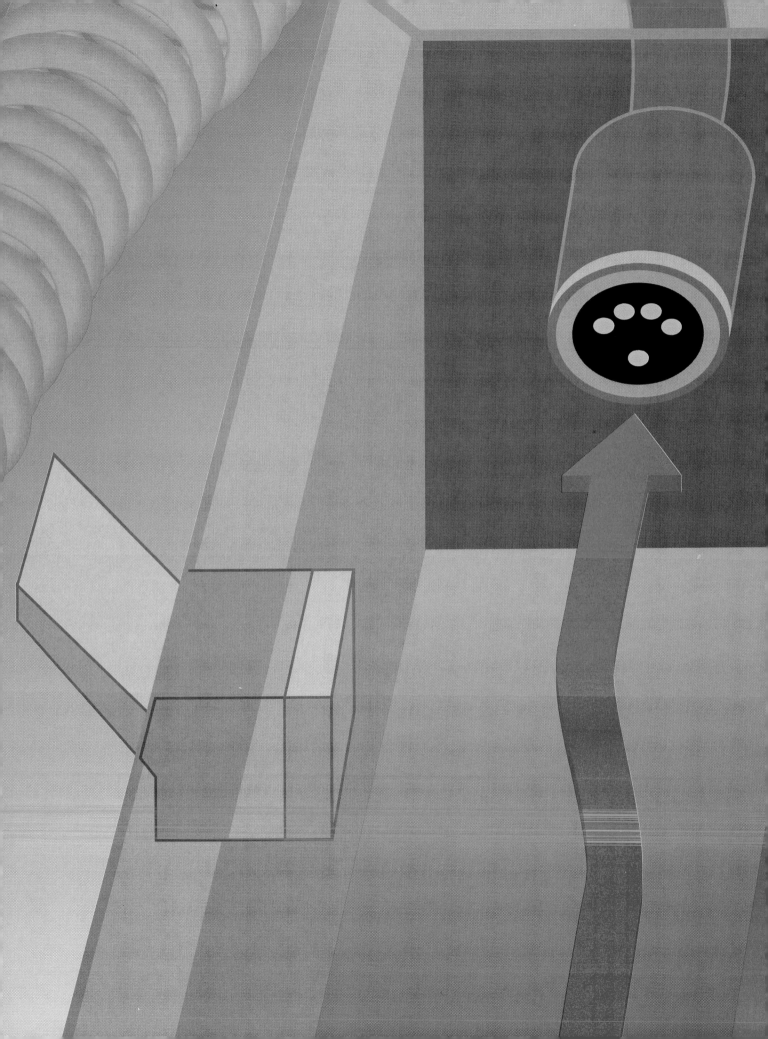

BOOT-UP PROCESS

OVERVIEW

WHEN YOUR PERSONAL computer is turned off, it is a dead collection of sheet metal, plastic, metallic tracings, and tiny flakes of silicon. When you hit the On switch, one little burst of electricity—only about five volts—starts a string of events that magically brings to life what otherwise would remain an oversize paperweight.

Even with that spark of life in it, however, the PC is still rather stupid at first. It has some primitive sense of self as it checks to see what parts are installed and working, like those patients who've awakened from a coma and check to make sure that they have all their arms and legs and that all their joints still work. But beyond taking inventory of itself, the newly awakened PC still can't do anything really useful, certainly nothing we'd even remotely think of as intelligent.

At best it can search for intelligence—intelligence in the form of an operating system that gives structure to the PC's primitive, amoebic existence. Then comes a true education in the form of application software—programs that tell it how to do tasks faster and more accurately than we could, a student who's outstripped its teacher.

But not all kinds of computers have to endure such a torturous rebirth each time they're turned on. You encounter daily many computers that spring to life fully formed at the instant they're switched on. You may not think of them as computers, but they are: calculators, your car's electronic ignition, the timer in the microwave, and the unfathomable programmer in your VCR. The difference between these and the big box on your desk is hard wiring. Computers built to accomplish only one task—and they are very efficient about doing that task—are hard-wired. But that means that they are more idiot savants than sages.

B O O T - U P
PROCESS

What makes your PC such a miraculous device is that each time you turn it on, it is a tabula rasa, capable of doing anything your creativity—or, more usually, the creativity of professional programmers—can imagine for it to do. It is a calculating machine, an artist's canvas, a magical typewriter, an unerring accountant, and a host of other tools. To transform it from one persona to another merely requires setting some of the microscopic switches buried in the hearts of the microchips, a task accomplished by typing a command at the DOS prompt or by clicking with your mouse on some tiny icon on the screen.

Such intelligence is fragile and short-lived. All those millions of microscopic switches are constantly flipping on and off in time to dashing surges of electricity. All it takes is an errant instruction or a stray misreading of a single switch to send this wonderfully intelligent golem into a state of catatonia. Or hit the Off switch and what was a pulsing artificial life dies without a whimper.

Then the next time you turn it on, birth begins all over again.

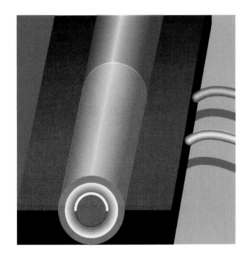

How the Power-On Self-Test Works

WHEN YOU HIT your PC's On switch, nothing much seems to happen for several seconds. Actually, your computer is going through a complex set of operations to make sure all of its components are working properly and to warn you if something's amiss. This operation is the first step in an even more complicated process called the *boot-up* or simply, the *boot*. The term comes from the idea of lifting yourself up by your own bootstraps. In a PC, bootstrapping is necessary because the PC has to have some way of bringing all its components to life long enough so that they can accomplish the goal of loading an operating system. The operating system then takes on more complicated tasks that the boot code alone can't manage, including making the PC's hardware interact with software.

But before your PC can even attempt to load an operating system, it has to make sure that all the hardware components are running and that the CPU (central processing unit) and memory are functioning properly. This is the job of the power-on self-test, or POST.

The POST is the first thing your PC does when you turn it on, and it's your first warning of trouble with any of the components. When the POST detects an error from the display, memory, keyboard, or other basic components, it produces an error warning in the form of a message on your display and—in case your display is part of the problem—in the form of a series of beeps. Usually neither the beeps nor the on-screen message is specific enough to tell you exactly what is wrong. All they're intended to do is to point you in the general direction of the component that has a problem.

A single beep combined with a display of the normal DOS prompt means that all components have passed the POST. But any other combination of shorts beeps and long beeps usually means trouble. Even no beep at all indicates a problem.

Here's a table that tells how to translate the beeps—(•) for short, (–) for long—or lack of them.

Beeps	Display	Problem Area
None	None	Power
None	Cursor only	Power
None	DOS prompt	Speaker
•	DOS prompt	Normal
•	BASIC screen	Disk
•–	None	Monitor
••	None	Monitor
••	Error code	Other, usually memory
Several •	305 error code	Keyboard
Several •	Anything else	Power
Continuous beep	Anything else	Power
–•	Anything else	System board
–••	Anything else	Monitor
–•••	Anything else	Monitor

If no error message appears or beeps occur, however, that doesn't mean all the hardware components of your system are functioning as they should. The POST is capable of detecting only the most general types of errors. It can tell if a hard drive that's supposed to be installed isn't there, but it can't tell if there is trouble with the drive's formatting.

All in all, the POST does not appear to be extremely helpful. That's because most PCs function so reliably that only rarely does anything trigger a POST alarm. The POST's benefits are subtle but fundamental. Without it, you could never be sure of the PC's ability to carry out its tasks accurately and reliably.

Power-On Self-Test

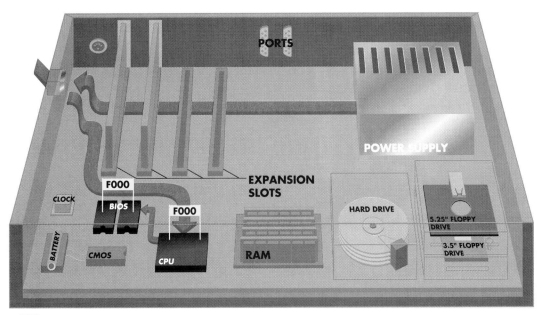

1 When you turn on your PC, an electrical signal follows a permanently programmed path to the CPU to clear leftover data from the chip's internal memory registers. The signal resets a CPU register called the program counter to a specific number. In the case of ATs and later computers, the number is F000. The number in the program counter tells the CPU the address of the next instruction that needs processing. In this case, the address is the beginning of a boot program stored permanently at the address F000 in a set of read-only memory (ROM) chips that contain the PC's basic input/output system (BIOS).

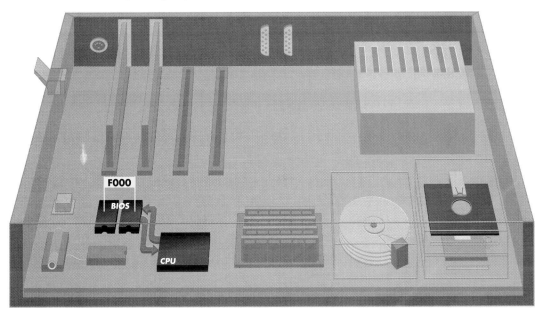

2 The CPU uses the address to find and invoke the ROM BIOS boot program, which in turn invokes a series of system checks, known as power-on self-tests, or POSTs. The CPU first checks itself and the POST program by reading code at various locations and checking it against identical permanent records. [*Continued on next page.*]

Power-On Self-Test

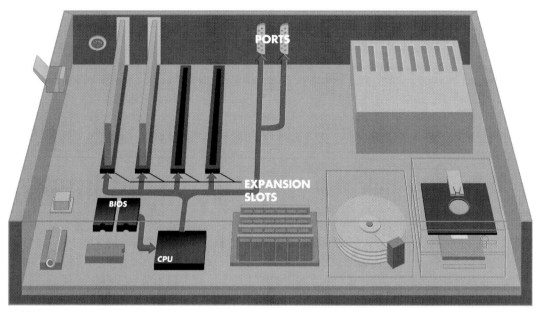

3 The CPU sends signals over the system *bus*—the circuits that connect all the components with each other—to make sure that they are all functioning.

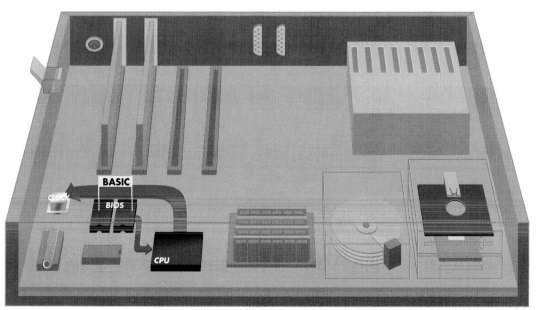

4 On older PCs that contain a kernel of the programming language BASIC in ROM, that section of code is checked while the CPU also checks the system's timer, which is responsible for making sure that all of the PC's operations function in a synchronized, orderly fashion.

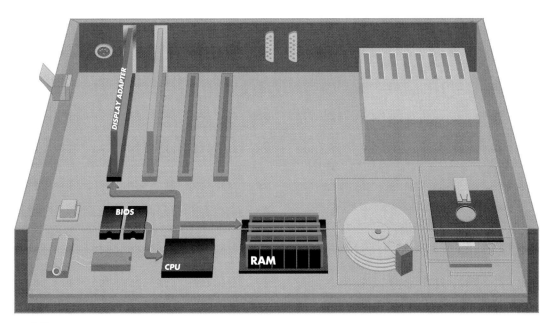

5 The POST procedure tests the memory contained on the display adapter and the video signals that control the display. It then makes the adapter's BIOS code a part of the system's overall BIOS and memory configuration. It's at this point that you'll first see something appear on your PC's monitor.

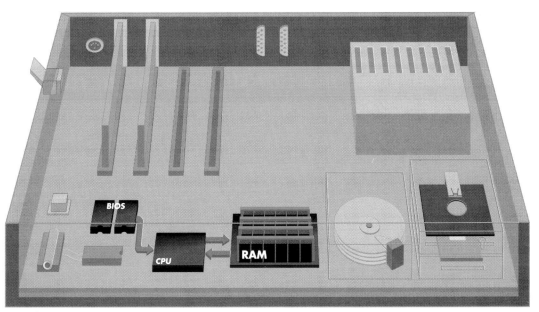

6 The POST runs a series of tests to ensure that the RAM chips are functioning properly. The CPU writes data to each chip, then reads it and compares what it reads with the data it sent to the chips in the first place. A running account of the amount of memory that's been checked is displayed on the monitor during this test. [*Continued on next page.*]

Power-On Self-Test

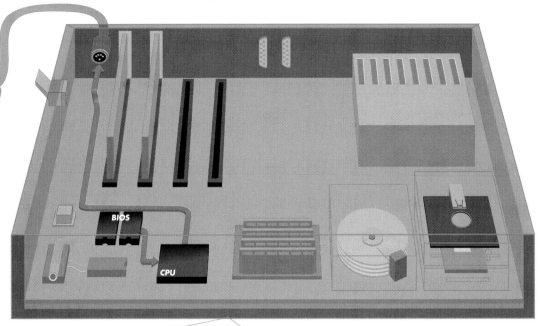

7 The CPU checks to make sure that the keyboard is attached properly and looks to see if any keys have been pressed.

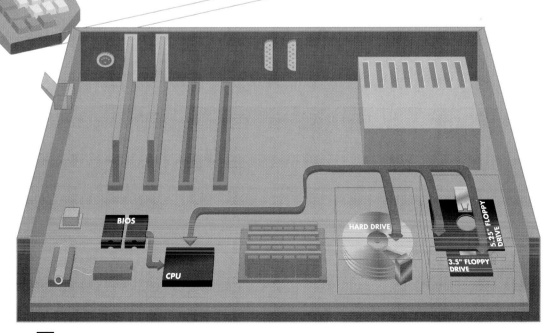

8 The POST sends signals over specific paths on the bus to any disk drives and listens for a response to determine what drives are available.

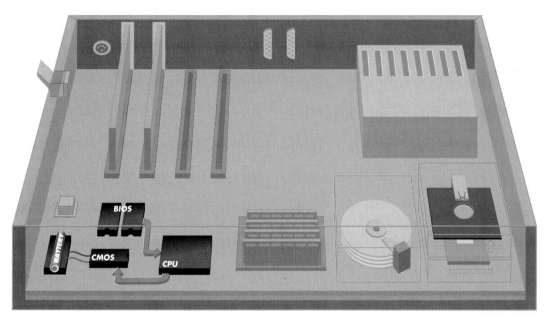

9 On AT class or later PCs, the results of the POST tests are compared with a record in a specific CMOS chip that is the official record of which components are installed. CMOS is a type of memory chip that retains its data when power is turned off as long as it receives a trickle of electricity from a battery. Any changes to the basic system configuration must be recorded in the CMOS setup data on all PCs that include that function. (Only the original PC and PC XT class of computers don't use a CMOS function.)

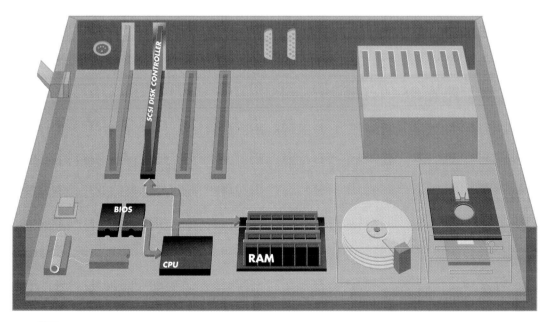

10 On systems that contain components that include their own BIOS, such as some disk controller cards, that BIOS code is recognized and incorporated as part of the system's own BIOS and memory use. The PC is now ready to take the next step in the boot process: loading an operating system from disk.

How a Disk Boot Works

APERSONAL COMPUTER can't do anything useful unless it's running an *operating system—* the software that lets the PC use other software. But before it can run an operating system, it needs some way to load the operating system from disk to random access memory (RAM). That way is with the *bootstrap* or simply, boot—a small amount of code that's permanently a part of the PC.

The bootstrap is aptly named because it lets the PC do something entirely on its own, without any outside operating system. Of course, the boot operation doesn't do very much. In fact, it has only two functions: one is to run a POST, or power-on self-test (described in the previous chapter), and the other is to search drives for an operating system. When these functions are complete, the boot operation launches the process of reading the operating system files and copying them to random access memory.

Why do PCs use such a roundabout arrangement? Why not simply make the operating system a part of the PC? A few low-end or specialized computers do this. Early computers used primarily for playing games, such as the Atari 400 and 800, and the recent Hewlett-Packard LX95 palmtop have a permanent operating system. The LX95 even includes an application program, Lotus 1-2-3, on a special microchip. But in most cases, the operating system is loaded from disk for two reasons.

It is simpler to upgrade the operating system when loading from a disk. When a company such as Microsoft—which makes MS-DOS, the most commonly used PC operating system—wants to add new features or fix serious bugs, it can simply issue a new set of disks. Sometimes all that's necessary is a single file that patches a flaw in the operating system. It's cheaper for Microsoft to distribute DOS on disk than to design a microchip that contains the operating system. And it's easier for computer users to install a new DOS from disk than it is to swap chips.

The other reason for loading an operating system from disk is that it gives users a choice of operating systems. Although most PCs based on microprocessors built by Intel use MS-DOS, there are alternative operating systems, such as OS/2, DR DOS, and Unix. In some PC set-ups, you can even choose which of the operating systems to use each time you turn on your computer.

Disk Boot

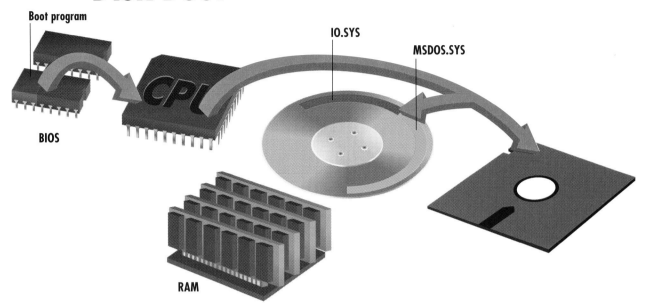

Boot program

IO.SYS

MSDOS.SYS

BIOS

RAM

1 After conducting a POST check of all the hardware components of a PC, the boot program contained on the computer's ROM BIOS chips checks drive A to see if it contains a formatted floppy disk. If a disk is mounted in the drive, the program searches specific locations on the disk for the files that make up the first two parts of the operating system. You won't ordinarily see these system files because each is marked with a special file attribute that hides it from the DOS DIR command. On most PCs, the files are named IO.SYS and MSDOS.SYS. On IBM computers, the files are named IBMBIO.COM and IBMDOS.COM. If the floppy drive is empty, the boot program checks the hard drive C for the system files. If a boot disk does not contain the files, the boot program generates an error message.

7C00

Boot record

2 After locating a disk with the system files, the boot program reads the data stored on the disk's first sector and copies that data to specific locations in RAM. This information constitutes the DOS *boot record*. The boot record is found in the same location on every formatted disk. The boot record is only about 512 bytes, just enough code to initiate the loading of the two hidden system files. After the BIOS boot program has loaded the boot record into memory at the hexadecimal address 7C00, the BIOS passes control to the boot record by branching to that address.

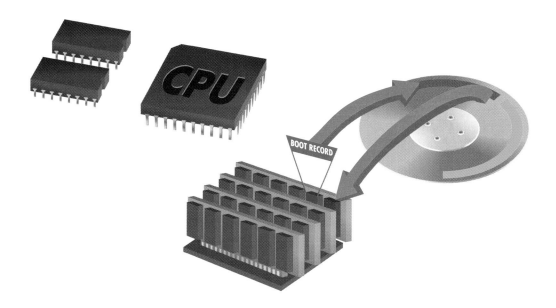

3 The boot record takes control of the PC and loads IO.SYS into RAM. The IO.SYS file contains extensions to the ROM BIOS and includes a routine called SYSINIT that manages the rest of the boot up. After loading IO.SYS, the boot record is no longer needed and is replaced in RAM by other code.

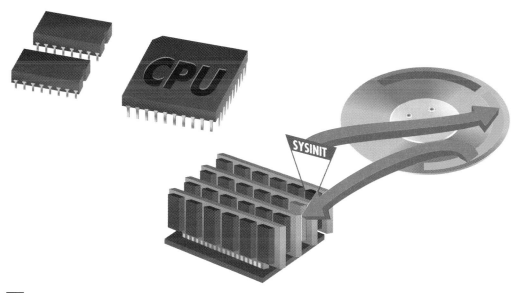

4 SYSINIT assumes control of the start-up process and loads MSDOS.SYS into RAM. The MSDOS.SYS file works with the BIOS to manage files, execute programs, and respond to signals from hardware. [*Continued on next page.*]

Disk Boot

FILES=50
BUFFERS=20
DEVICE= HIMEM.SYS
DEVICE=RAMDRIVE.SYS

SYSINIT

MSDOS.SYS

CONFIG.SYS

5 SYSINIT searches the root directory of the boot disk for a file named CONFIG.SYS. If CONFIG-
.SYS exists, SYSINIT tells MSDOS.SYS to execute the commands in the file. CONFIG.SYS is a
file created by the user. Its commands tell the operating system how to handle certain operations,
such as how many files may be opened at one time. CONFIG.SYS may also contain instructions to
load device drivers. *Device drivers* are files containing code that extends the capabilities of the BIOS
to control memory or hardware devices.

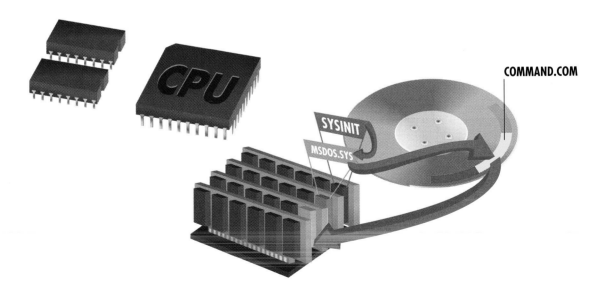

COMMAND.COM

SYSINIT

MSDOS.SYS

6 SYSINIT tells MSDOS.SYS to load the file COMMAND.COM. This operating system file consists
of three parts. One is a further extension to the input/output functions. This part is loaded in memory with the BIOS and becomes a permanent part of the operating system.

7 The second part of COMMAND.COM contains the internal DOS commands such as DIR, COPY, and TYPE. It is loaded at the high end of conventional RAM, where it can be overwritten by applications programs if they need the memory.

8 The third part of COMMAND.COM is used only once and then discarded. This part searches the root directory for a file named AUTOEXEC.BAT. This file is created by the computer's user and contains a series of DOS batch file commands and/or the names of programs that the user wants to run each time the computer is turned on. The PC is now fully booted and ready to be used.

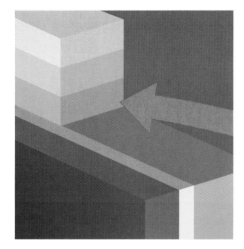

CHAPTER 3

How an Operating System Works

THE NAME OF the most popular operating system for Intel-based PCs—MS-DOS—stands for *Microsoft disk operating system*. Originally, operating systems were envisioned as a way to handle one of the most complex input/output operations: communicating with a variety of disk drives. But, the operating system quickly evolved into an all-encompassing bridge between your PC and the software you run on it.

Without an operating system, each programmer would have to invent from scratch how a program would display text or graphics on screen, how it would send data to the printer, how it would read or write disk files, and a multitude of other functions that mesh software with hardware. An operating system, however, is more than a way to make life easier for programmers.

An operating system creates a common platform for all the software you use. Without an operating system, you might not be able to save files created by two different programs to the same disk because each might have its own format for how those files are stored. An operating system also gives you a tool for all the tasks you want to perform outside of an application program—deleting and copying files, displaying file lists, and running a collection of commands in a batch file.

The operating system does not work alone. It depends not only on the cooperation of other programs, but on meshing smoothly with the BIOS. As seen in the previous chapter, when some parts of the operating system are loaded from disk, they are added to the BIOS and then joined by device drivers, and all of them carry out routine hardware functions. The operating system is really composed of all three of these components. It is simplistic to think of an operating system as being only the files contained on a certain disk that came with your PC.

Together the BIOS, device drivers, and operating system perform so many functions that it's impossible to depict their complexity with a couple of pages of illustrations. Here we'll show how memory is used by the operating system and provide a typical, simple example of software using a BIOS service to print a single character.

Operating System: Memory

2 The first kilobyte—1,024 bytes—holds *interrupt vectors* set by both the BIOS and DOS; these may be modified by application programs. The vectors point to the locations of software routines in other memory addresses to which operations should branch when various hardware components send a special signal called an interrupt.

3 The next 256 or so bytes contain BIOS data called *flags* that are used to indicate the state of various internal system conditions. Also in this area is a 16-byte *keyboard buffer* where keystrokes are stored while the PC is temporarily too busy with other tasks to process the keystrokes.

1 When MS-DOS is loaded on a PC, different parts of the operating system are assigned to different locations in a 1MB memory range that begins at address 0000. The range is a logically continuous map. But the actual physical locations of some of the addresses may be in different parts of the PC—in the ROM chips that contain the PC's BIOS, in the BIOS chip on a display adapter card, in RAM chips on the PC's motherboard, or in memory chips on an expansion board.

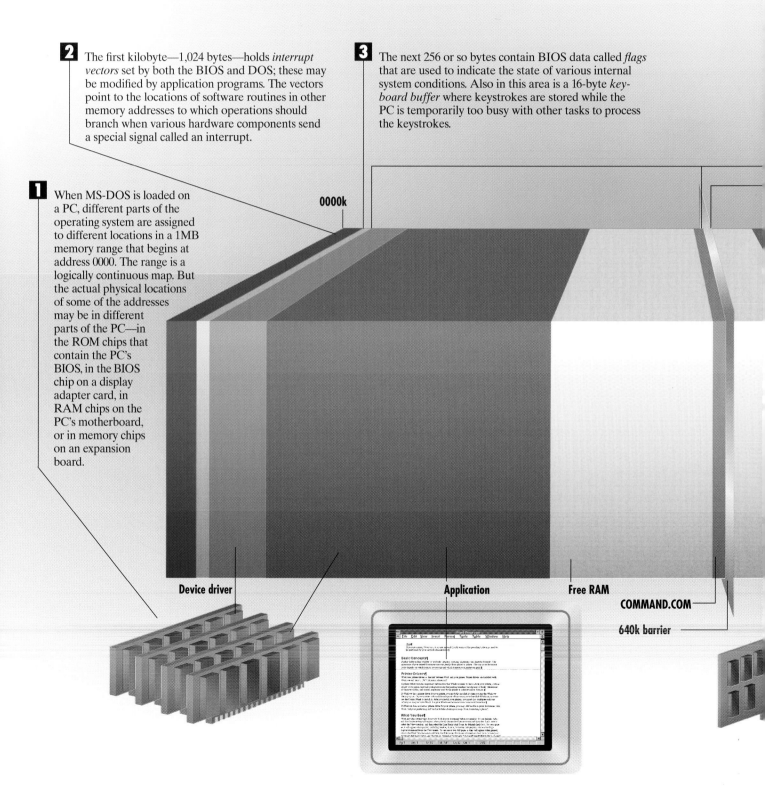

0000k

Device driver

Application

Free RAM

COMMAND.COM

640k barrier

4 The rest of RAM, up to 640k, constitutes *ordinary memory*. This is the RAM into which COMMAND.COM, device drivers, memory-resident programs, and application software are ordinarily loaded. Memory managers, such as QEMM-386 or HIMEM.SYS provided with newer versions of MS-DOS, permit remapping of memory so that device drivers, memory-resident programs and, in DOS 5.0 or later, part of COMMAND.COM can be loaded in high memory, above the 640k reserved for application software. If such a memory manager is not used, COMMAND.COM is loaded in the highest addresses within ordinary memory, where it may be overwritten by any application software that needs the memory.

5 Above ordinary memory is high memory, part of which is reserved for BIOS use by various types of display adapters, and for such adapters as network cards and hard-drive controllers. Memory managers can remap the areas assigned to these devices to create larger areas of unused memory, in which the memory managers then load other device drivers and programs.

1024k

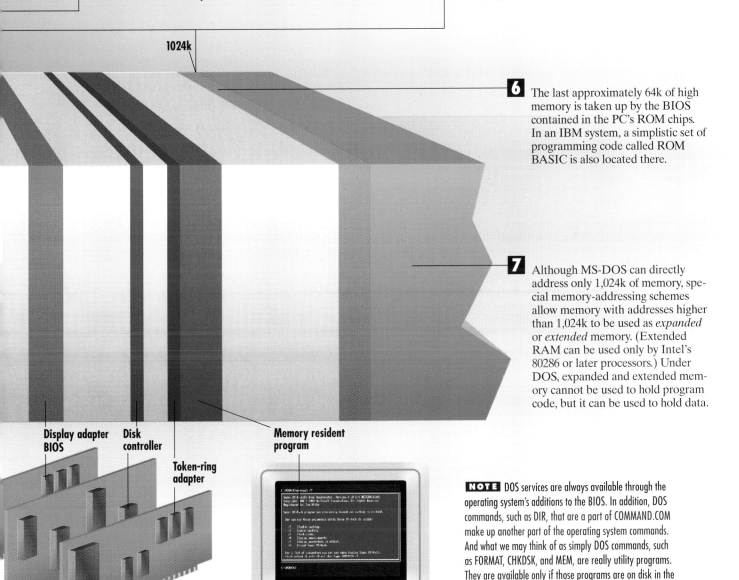

6 The last approximately 64k of high memory is taken up by the BIOS contained in the PC's ROM chips. In an IBM system, a simplistic set of programming code called ROM BASIC is also located there.

7 Although MS-DOS can directly address only 1,024k of memory, special memory-addressing schemes allow memory with addresses higher than 1,024k to be used as *expanded* or *extended* memory. (Extended RAM can be used only by Intel's 80286 or later processors.) Under DOS, expanded and extended memory cannot be used to hold program code, but it can be used to hold data.

Display adapter BIOS

Disk controller

Token-ring adapter

Memory resident program

NOTE DOS services are always available through the operating system's additions to the BIOS. In addition, DOS commands, such as DIR, that are a part of COMMAND.COM make up another part of the operating system commands. And what we may think of as simply DOS commands, such as FORMAT, CHKDSK, and MEM, are really utility programs. They are available only if those programs are on disk in the current directory or in one of the directories in a PC's path.

Operating System:
Software and Hardware

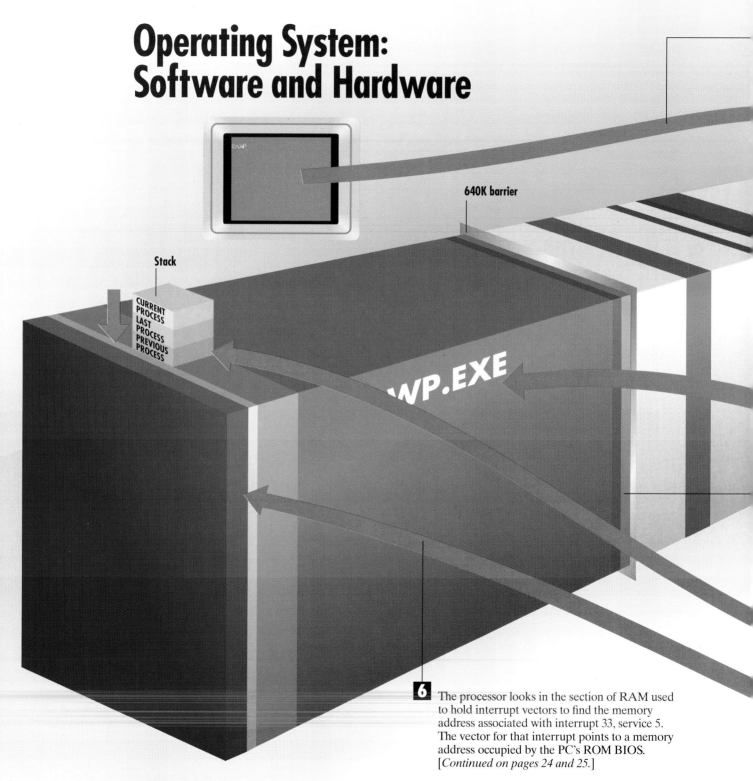

640K barrier

Stack

CURRENT
PROCESS
LAST
PROCESS
PREVIOUS
PROCESS

WP.EXE

6 The processor looks in the section of RAM used
to hold interrupt vectors to find the memory
address associated with interrupt 33, service 5.
The vector for that interrupt points to a memory
address occupied by the PC's ROM BIOS.
[*Continued on pages 24 and 25.*]

NOTE In some PC setups, a print spooler might be used to speed up printing. In that case, when the spooler
was loaded, it would have changed the vector for interrupt 33, service 5, to point to a routine in RAM used by
the spooler. The routine, typically, might have instructed the processor to send the character to a buffer area in
extended RAM, where it waits until the spooler's own routines send the character to the printer.

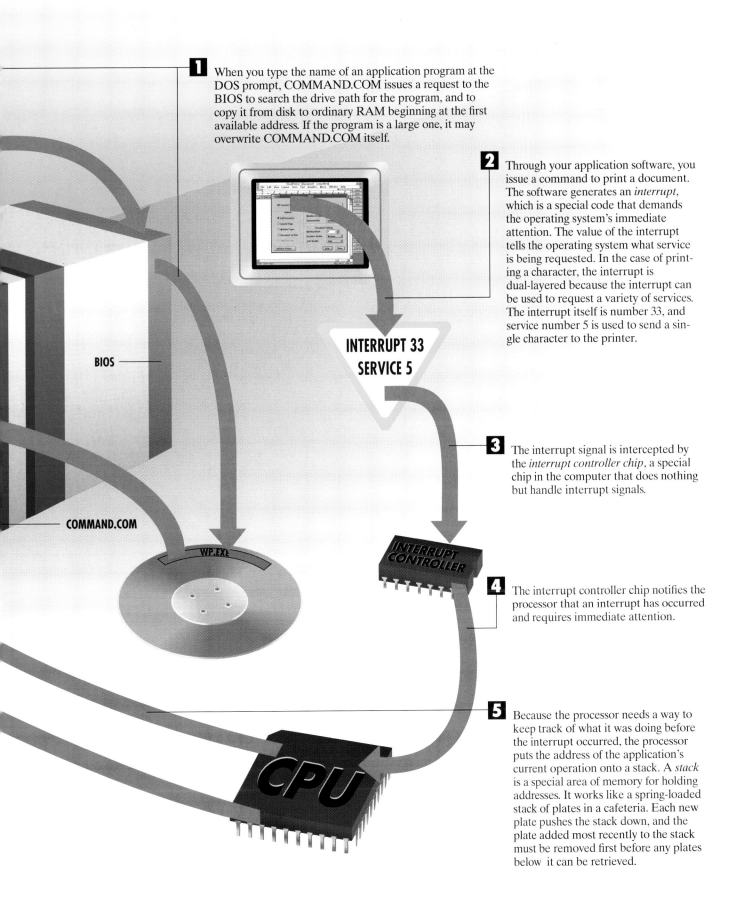

1 When you type the name of an application program at the DOS prompt, COMMAND.COM issues a request to the BIOS to search the drive path for the program, and to copy it from disk to ordinary RAM beginning at the first available address. If the program is a large one, it may overwrite COMMAND.COM itself.

2 Through your application software, you issue a command to print a document. The software generates an *interrupt*, which is a special code that demands the operating system's immediate attention. The value of the interrupt tells the operating system what service is being requested. In the case of printing a character, the interrupt is dual-layered because the interrupt can be used to request a variety of services. The interrupt itself is number 33, and service number 5 is used to send a single character to the printer.

INTERRUPT 33 SERVICE 5

BIOS

COMMAND.COM

WP.EXE

3 The interrupt signal is intercepted by the *interrupt controller chip*, a special chip in the computer that does nothing but handle interrupt signals.

INTERRUPT CONTROLLER

4 The interrupt controller chip notifies the processor that an interrupt has occurred and requires immediate attention.

CPU

5 Because the processor needs a way to keep track of what it was doing before the interrupt occurred, the processor puts the address of the application's current operation onto a stack. A *stack* is a special area of memory for holding addresses. It works like a spring-loaded stack of plates in a cafeteria. Each new plate pushes the stack down, and the plate added most recently to the stack must be removed first before any plates below it can be retrieved.

Operating System: Software and Hardware

Stack

LAST
PROCESS
PREVIOUS
PROCESS
PREVIOUS
PROCESS

WP.EXE

COMMAND.COM

COMMAND.COM

11 If the application program overwrote COMMAND.COM when the program was loaded, the operating system restores COMMAND.COM from disk to RAM when the application program is terminated.

10 The processor branches execution to the address obtained from the stack. The address is the location of the software routine that the computer was executing when the interrupt 33 occurred. By branching to that address, the processor picks up execution where it left off.

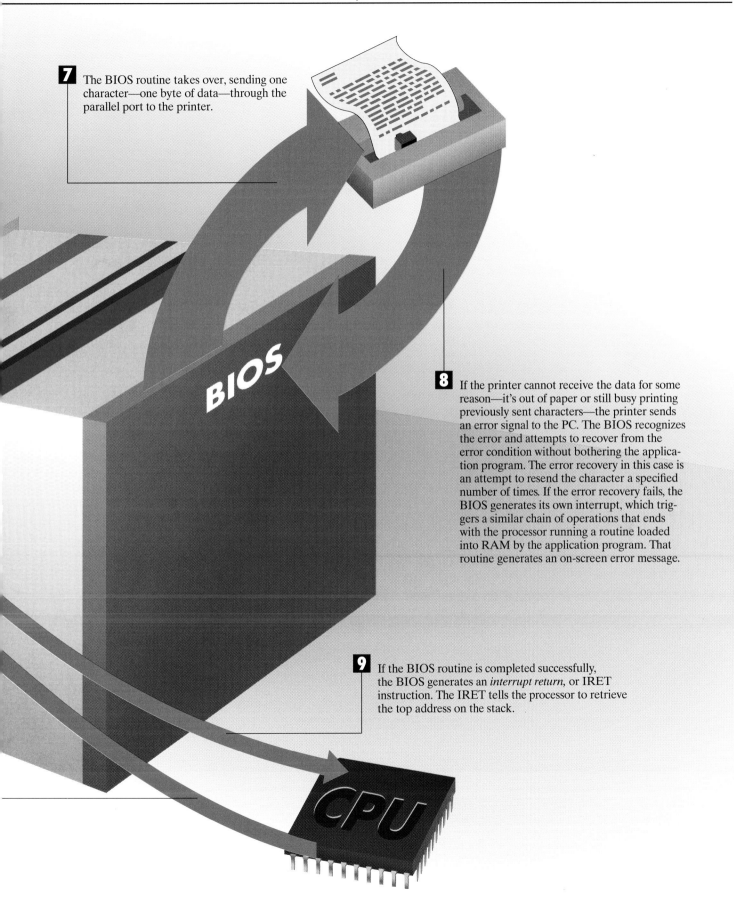

7 The BIOS routine takes over, sending one character—one byte of data—through the parallel port to the printer.

8 If the printer cannot receive the data for some reason—it's out of paper or still busy printing previously sent characters—the printer sends an error signal to the PC. The BIOS recognizes the error and attempts to recover from the error condition without bothering the application program. The error recovery in this case is an attempt to resend the character a specified number of times. If the error recovery fails, the BIOS generates its own interrupt, which triggers a similar chain of operations that ends with the processor running a routine loaded into RAM by the application program. That routine generates an on-screen error message.

9 If the BIOS routine is completed successfully, the BIOS generates an *interrupt return*, or IRET instruction. The IRET tells the processor to retrieve the top address on the stack.

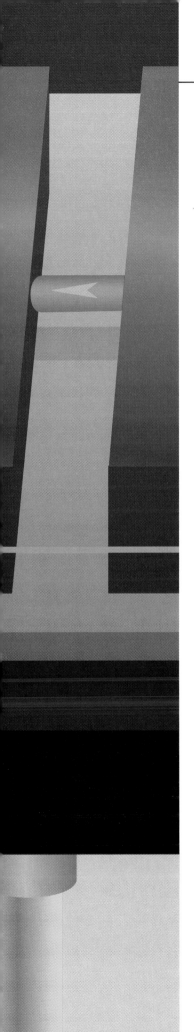

MICROCHIPS

CONTENTS

THE FIRST COMPUTERS used components called vacuum tubes. If you're not at least old enough to be part of the baby boom generation, you may never have seen more than one type of vacuum tube. They are no longer used in any electronic device, except for the gigantic vacuum tubes in your PC monitor and your TV screen.

Vacuum tubes functioned as electronic switches. When current flowed through one part of the tube, it made another component so hot that electrons boiled off and were attracted to a part of the tube that had a positive charge. A partial vacuum was needed inside the tube so that the electrons would encounter little resistance from molecules in air. When the electrons were flowing, the switch was on. When they weren't flowing, the switch was off.

Essentially a computer is just a collection of On/Off switches, which at first doesn't seem very useful. But imagine a large array of light bulbs—say, ten rows that each have 50 light bulbs in them. Each bulb is connected to a light switch. If you turn on the right combination of light bulbs, you can put your name in lights.

Computers are very similar to that bank of lights, with one important difference: A computer can sense which light bulbs are on and use that information to turn on other switches. If the pattern of On switches spells *Tom,* then the computer could be programmed to associate the *Tom* pattern with instructions to turn on another group of switches to spell *boy.* If the pattern spells *Mary,* the computer could turn on a different group of switches to spell *girl.* The two-pronged concept of On and Off maps perfectly with the binary number system, which uses only 0 and 1 to represent all numbers. By manipulating a roomful of vacuum tubes, early computer engineers could perform binary mathematical calculations, and by assigning alphanumeric characters to certain numbers, they could manipulate text.

The problem with those first computers, however, was that the intense heat generated by the hundreds of vacuum tubes made them notoriously unreliable. The heat caused many components to deteriorate and consumed enormous amounts of power. But for vacuum tubes to be on, the tubes didn't really need to generate the immense flow of electrons that they created. A small flow would do quite nicely, but vacuum tubes were big. They worked on a human scale in which each part could be seen with the naked eye. They were simply too crude to produce more subtle flows of electrons. Transistors changed the way computers could be built.

A transistor is essentially a vacuum tube built, not on a human scale, but on a microscopic scale. Because it is small, it requires less power to generate a flow of electrons. Because it uses less power, a transistor generates less heat, making computers more dependable. And the microscopic scale of transistors means that a computer that once took up an entire room now fits neatly on your lap.

All microchips, whether they're microprocessors, a memory chip, or a special-purpose integrated circuit, are basically vast collections of transistors arranged in different patterns so that they accomplish different tasks. Currently, the number of transistors that can be created on a single chip is about 1.5 million. The physical limitation is caused by how narrowly manufacturers can focus the beams of light used to etch away transistor components made of light-sensitive materials. Chip makers are experimenting with X rays instead of ordinary light because X rays are much narrower. Someday, transistors may be taken to their logical extreme—the molecular level, in which the presence or absence of just one electron signals an On or Off state.

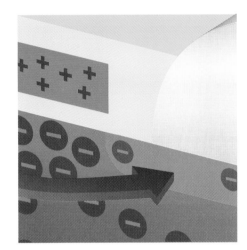

How a Transistor Works

THE TRANSISTOR IS the basic building block from which all microchips are built. The transistor can only create binary information: a 1 if current passes through or a 0 if current doesn't. From these 1s and 0s, called *bits*, a computer can create any number, provided it has enough transistors grouped together to hold the 1s and 0s required.

Binary notation starts off simply enough:

Decimal Number	Binary Number	Decimal Number	Binary Number
0	0	6	110
1	1	7	111
2	10	8	1000
3	11	9	1001
4	100	10	1010
5	101		

Personal computers such as those based on the Intel 8088 and 80286 microprocessors are 16-bit PCs. That means they can work directly with binary numbers of up to 16 places or bits. That translates to the decimal number 65,536. If an operation requires numbers larger than that, the PC must first break those numbers into smaller components, perform the operation on each of the components, and then recombine the results into a single answer. More powerful PCs, such as those based on the Intel 80386 and 80486, are 32-bit computers, which means they can manipulate binary numbers up to 32 bits wide—the equivalent in decimal notation of 4,294,967,296. The ability to work with 32 bits at a time helps make these PCs so much faster.

Transistors are not used simply to record and manipulate numbers. The bits can just as easily stand for true (1) or not true (0), which allows computers to deal with Boolean logic. Combinations of transistors in various configurations are called *logic gates*, which are combined into arrays called *half-adders*, which in turn are combined into *full adders*. More than 260 transistors are needed to create a full adder that can handle mathematical operations for 16-bit numbers.

In addition, transistors make it possible for a small amount of electrical current to control a second, much stronger current—just as the small amount of energy needed to throw a wall switch can control the more powerful energy surging through the wires to a light.

Transistor

1 A small positive electrical charge is sent down one aluminum lead that runs into the transistor. The positive charge is transferred to a layer of conductive polysilicon buried in the middle of nonconductive silicon dioxide.

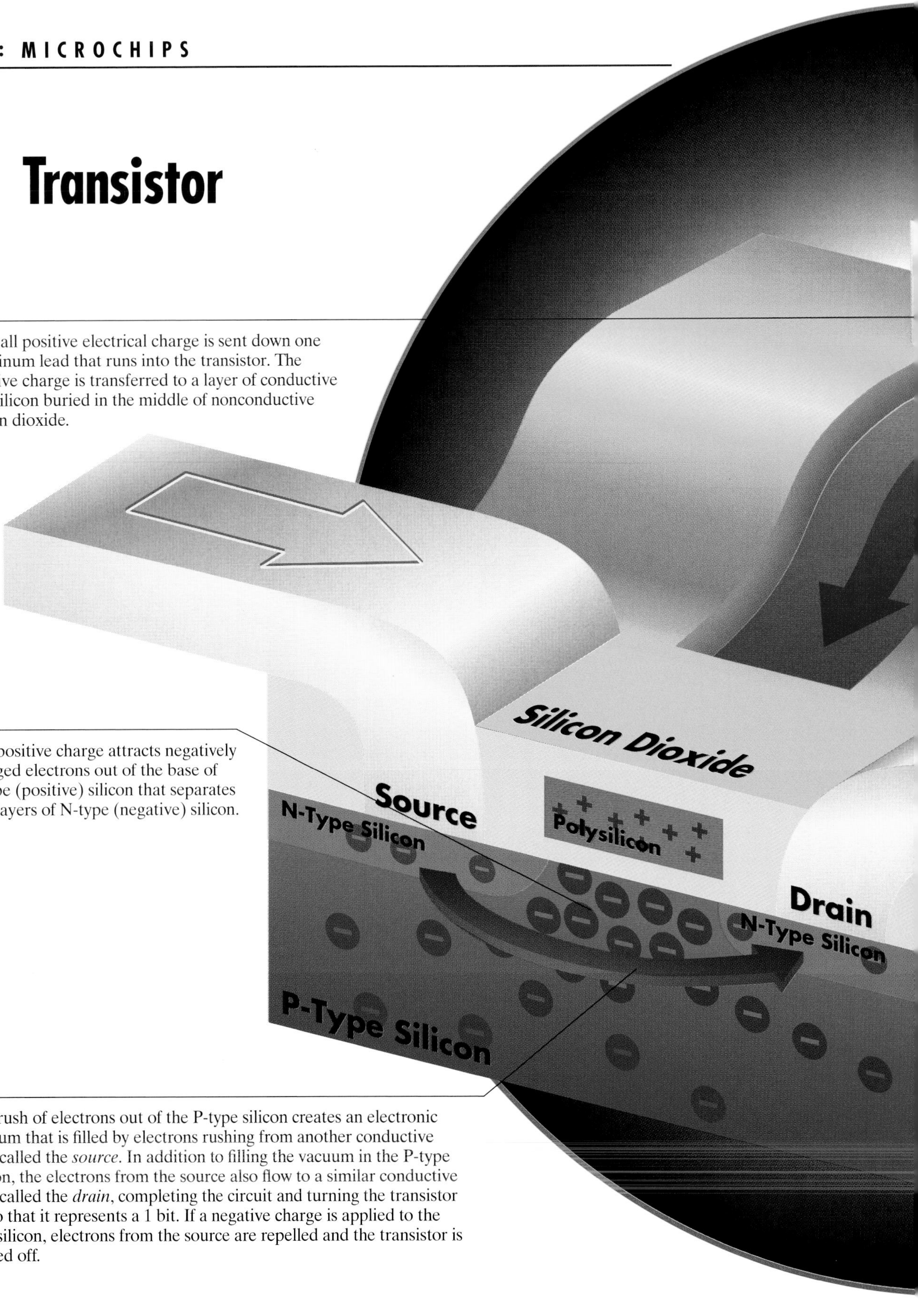

2 The positive charge attracts negatively charged electrons out of the base of P-type (positive) silicon that separates two layers of N-type (negative) silicon.

Silicon Dioxide

Source
N-Type Silicon

Polysilicon

Drain
N-Type Silicon

P-Type Silicon

3 The rush of electrons out of the P-type silicon creates an electronic vacuum that is filled by electrons rushing from another conductive lead called the *source*. In addition to filling the vacuum in the P-type silicon, the electrons from the source also flow to a similar conductive lead called the *drain*, completing the circuit and turning the transistor on so that it represents a 1 bit. If a negative charge is applied to the polysilicon, electrons from the source are repelled and the transistor is turned off.

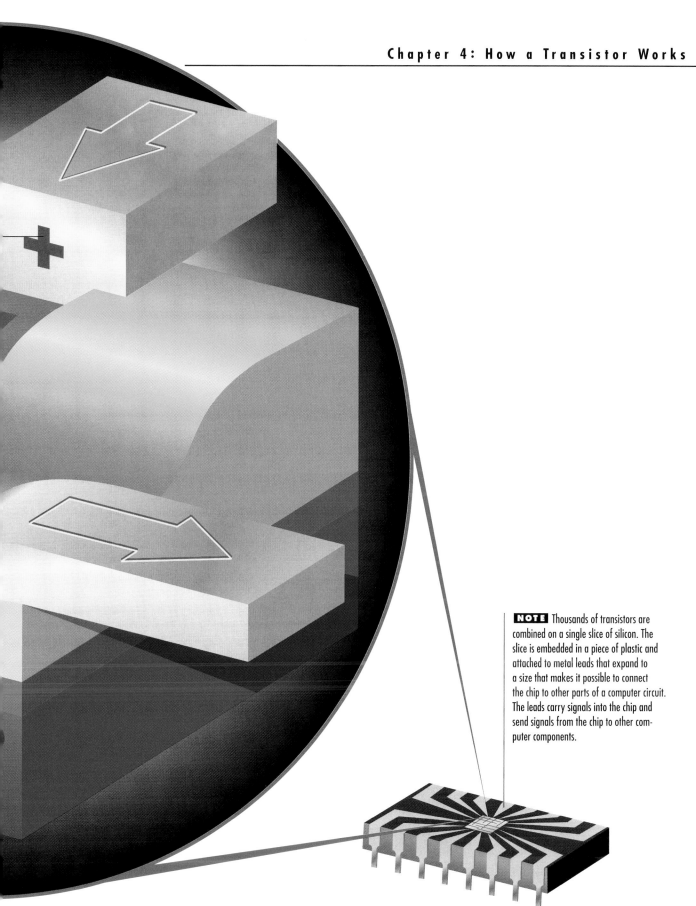

NOTE Thousands of transistors are combined on a single slice of silicon. The slice is embedded in a piece of plastic and attached to metal leads that expand to a size that makes it possible to connect the chip to other parts of a computer circuit. The leads carry signals into the chip and send signals from the chip to other computer components.

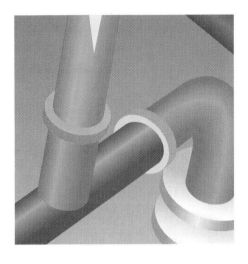

How RAM Works

RANDOM ACCESS MEMORY (RAM) chips are to your computer what a blank canvas is to an artist. Before a PC can do anything useful, it must move programs from disk to RAM. The data contained in documents, spreadsheets, graphics, databases, or any type of file must also be stored in RAM, if only momentarily, before the software can use the processor to manipulate that data.

Regardless of what kind of data a personal computer is using and regardless of how complex that data may appear to us, to the PC, that data exists only as 0s and 1s. Binary numbers are the native tongue of computers because even the biggest, most powerful computer essentially is no more than a collection of switches: An open switch represents a 0; a closed switch represents a 1. This is sometimes referred to as a computer's machine language. From this simplest of all numeric systems, your computer can construct representations of millions of numbers, any word in any language, and hundreds of thousands of colors and shapes.

Because humans are not nearly as fluent at binary notation as computers are, all those binary numbers appear on screen in some understandable notation—usually the alphabet or decimal numbers. For example, when you type an uppercase *A*, the operating system and software use a convention known as *ASCII*, in which certain numbers represent certain letters. A computer is essentially a number manipulator, which is why it's easier at the machine level for computers to deal with binary numbers. But it's easier for programmers and other humans to use decimal numbers. The capital *A* is the decimal number 65; *B* is 66; *C* is 67; and so on. Still, in the heart of a computer, the numbers are stored in their binary equivalents.

It is these binary notations that fill your disks and the PC's memory. But when you first turn on your computer, its RAM is a blank slate. The memory is filled with 0s and 1s that are read from disk or created by the work you do with the computer. When you turn off your PC, anything that's contained in RAM disappears. Some newer forms of RAM chips retain their electrical charges when a computer is turned off. But most memory chips work only if there is a source of electricity to constantly refresh the thousands or millions of individual electrical charges that make up the programs and data stored in RAM.

Writing Data to RAM

3 While the transistors are turned on, the software sends bursts of electricity along selected data lines. Each burst represents a *bit*—either a 1 or a 0, in the native language of processors, and the ultimate unit of information that a computer manipulates.

2 At each memory location in a RAM chip where data can be stored, the electrical pulse turns on (closes) a transistor that's connected to a data line. A *transistor* is essentially a microscopic electrical switch.

1 Software in combination with DOS sends a burst of electricity along an *address line*, which is a microscopic strand of electrically conductive material etched onto a RAM chip. This burst identifies where to record data among the many address lines in a RAM chip.

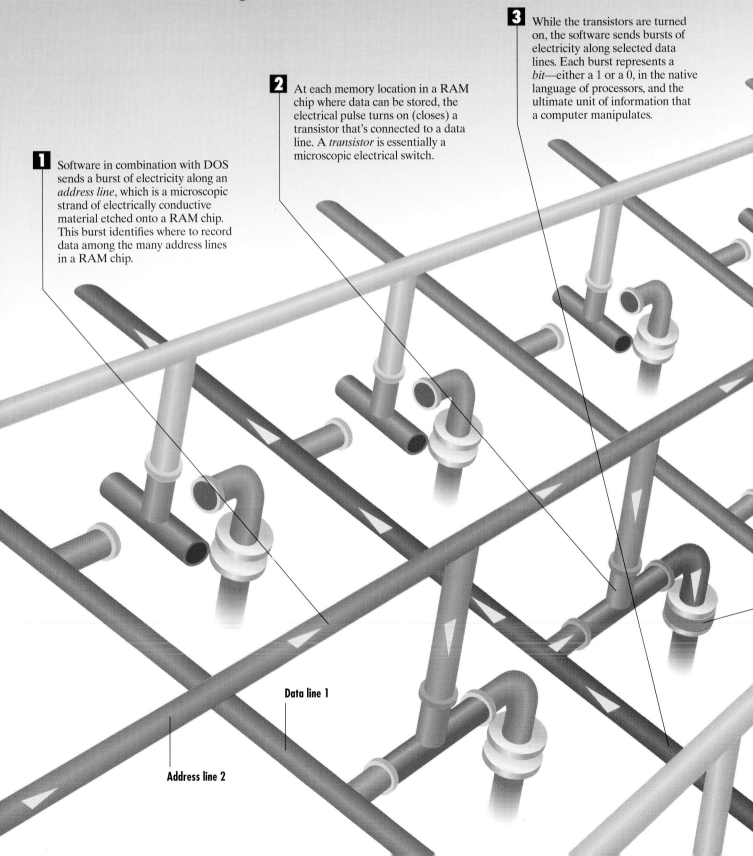

Data line 1

Address line 2

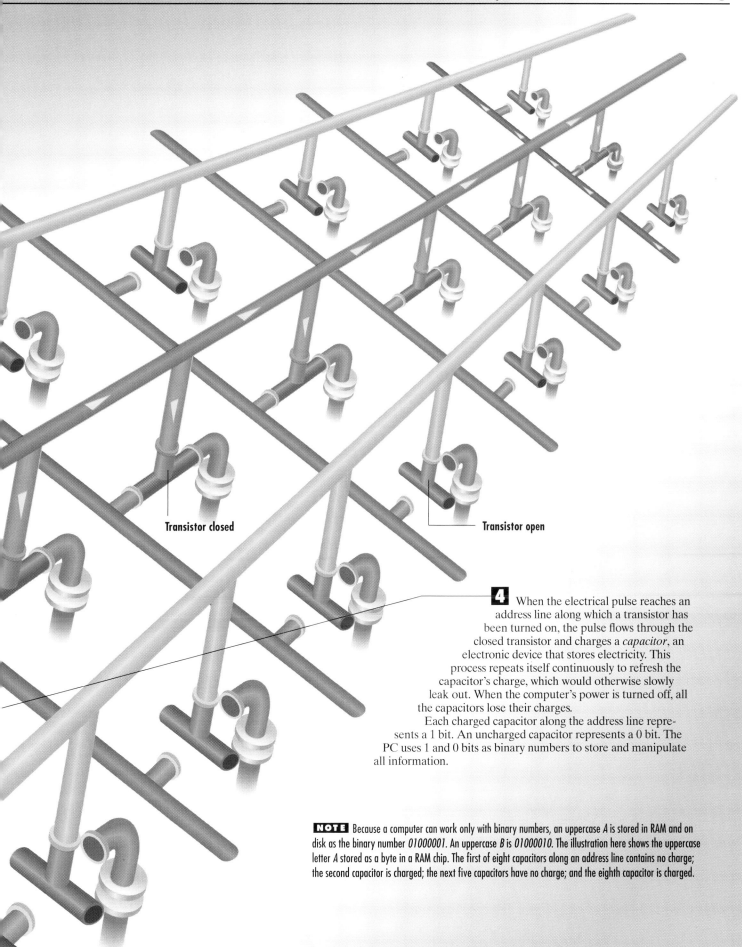

Transistor closed

Transistor open

4 When the electrical pulse reaches an address line along which a transistor has been turned on, the pulse flows through the closed transistor and charges a *capacitor*, an electronic device that stores electricity. This process repeats itself continuously to refresh the capacitor's charge, which would otherwise slowly leak out. When the computer's power is turned off, all the capacitors lose their charges.

Each charged capacitor along the address line represents a 1 bit. An uncharged capacitor represents a 0 bit. The PC uses 1 and 0 bits as binary numbers to store and manipulate all information.

NOTE Because a computer can work only with binary numbers, an uppercase *A* is stored in RAM and on disk as the binary number *01000001*. An uppercase *B* is *01000010*. The illustration here shows the uppercase letter *A* stored as a byte in a RAM chip. The first of eight capacitors along an address line contains no charge; the second capacitor is charged; the next five capacitors have no charge; and the eighth capacitor is charged.

Reading Data from RAM

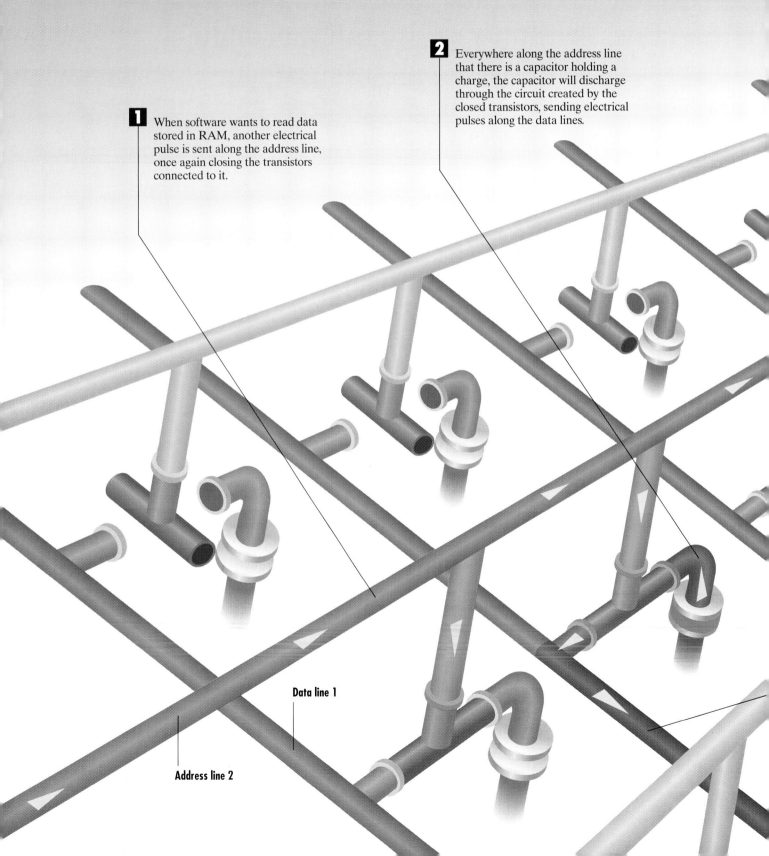

2 Everywhere along the address line that there is a capacitor holding a charge, the capacitor will discharge through the circuit created by the closed transistors, sending electrical pulses along the data lines.

1 When software wants to read data stored in RAM, another electrical pulse is sent along the address line, once again closing the transistors connected to it.

Data line 1

Address line 2

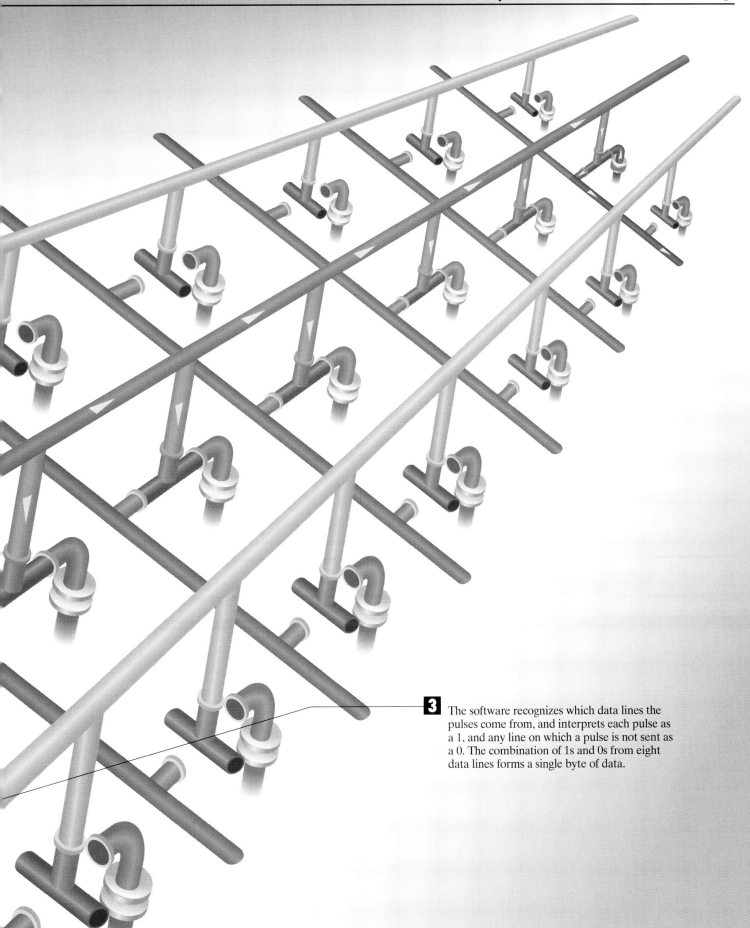

3 The software recognizes which data lines the pulses come from, and interprets each pulse as a 1, and any line on which a pulse is not sent as a 0. The combination of 1s and 0s from eight data lines forms a single byte of data.

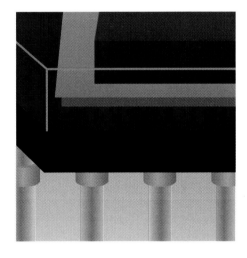

How a Microprocessor Works

ALTHOUGH INTEL'S 80386 microprocessor—the first 32-bit processor to be used in MS-DOS–based personal computers—is not the most powerful processor used in current PCs, it remains important because it creates a minimum standard for computing abilities. Because it can manipulate up to 32 bits of data at one time, it processes instructions two to three times as fast as its predecessor, the 80286, which in turn is at least five times as fast as the Intel 8088, the chip in the original IBM PC that sparked the personal computer revolution.

But speed is not the only advantage to the 80386. It includes specific instruction sets for managing memory, making it possible for an operating system to safely run several programs at the same time through a feature called *protected mode*. Another facility, *virtual 8086 mode*, allows additional protection because several programs running in that mode think they're running on a stand-alone 8088 PC. The software may act as if it's free to take some favorite shortcut to access a PC's hardware directly, but the 80386 intercepts those shortcuts and routes them through acceptable pathways so they don't interfere with other programs that also think they own the PC.

The six basic units of the 80386 obtain data and instructions from memory, store both where other units can get to them readily, make sense of the instructions, then carry out the instructions, and deliver the result back to RAM. Your own desk is an analogy for the workings of the 80386. The equivalent of the code and data that the chip works with are the reports and other papers deposited in your In basket. For example, in your In basket is a request from your boss for a report and the market data that you'll use in the report. Because you're busy doing something else when the request appears, you place it on a stack of pending work. When you're through with the current job, you retrieve the request and data and then carry out your boss's instructions. Then, you attach a distribution list to the report and put it in your Out basket. But the microprocessor is more efficient than you at doing these tasks because it performs them simultaneously. The individual steps correspond to the jobs performed by the 386's Bus Interface Unit, the Code Prefetch Unit, the Instruction Decode Unit, the Execution Unit, and the Segment and Paging units.

The example here shows how those parts work together to perform the simple addition of 2 + 2.

Microprocessor

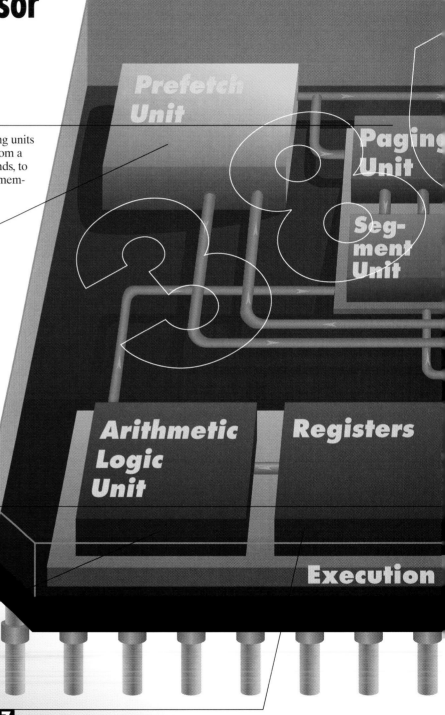

2 At the same time, the Segment and Paging units convert the location of that instruction from a virtual address, which software understands, to a physical address (an actual location in memory), which the Bus Interface Unit understands.

1 The Prefetch Unit, which queues instructions for processing, asks the Bus Interface Unit to retrieve from memory the next instruction—in our example, a command to add two numbers. The goal of the Prefetch Unit is to make sure that the Instruction Decode Unit won't have idle time while it waits for its next instruction.

9 The Control Unit tells the Bus Interface Unit to store the sum in RAM. The Segment and Paging units translate the virtual address specified by the Control Unit for that sum into a physical address, completing the instruction.

8 The Arithmetic Logic Unit, which is the microprocessor's calculator, produces the sum of the number that was just retrieved from RAM and the first number that had been stored in the internal registers.

7 The Bus Interface Unit locates and retrieves the number stored at that address. The number travels back through the Protection Test Unit to the Execution Unit, where it is stored in one of the chip's internal registers. The registers function as a combination scratch pad and working memory for the Execution Unit. A similar operation results in the second number also being fetched to the Execution Unit.

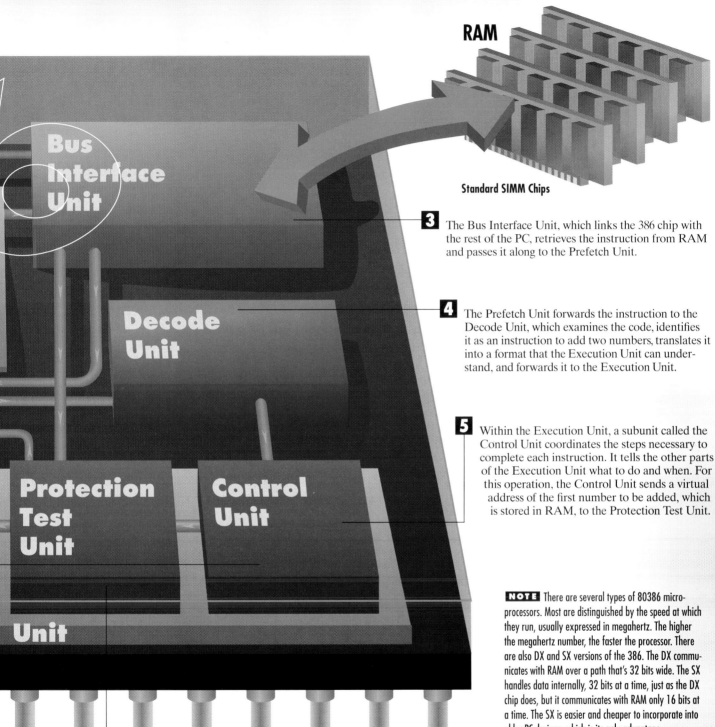

RAM

Standard SIMM Chips

3 The Bus Interface Unit, which links the 386 chip with the rest of the PC, retrieves the instruction from RAM and passes it along to the Prefetch Unit.

4 The Prefetch Unit forwards the instruction to the Decode Unit, which examines the code, identifies it as an instruction to add two numbers, translates it into a format that the Execution Unit can understand, and forwards it to the Execution Unit.

5 Within the Execution Unit, a subunit called the Control Unit coordinates the steps necessary to complete each instruction. It tells the other parts of the Execution Unit what to do and when. For this operation, the Control Unit sends a virtual address of the first number to be added, which is stored in RAM, to the Protection Test Unit.

NOTE There are several types of 80386 microprocessors. Most are distinguished by the speed at which they run, usually expressed in megahertz. The higher the megahertz number, the faster the processor. There are also DX and SX versions of the 386. The DX communicates with RAM over a path that's 32 bits wide. The SX handles data internally, 32 bits at a time, just as the DX chip does, but it communicates with RAM only 16 bits at a time. The SX is easier and cheaper to incorporate into older PC designs, which is its only advantage.

Since the 386 was released, Intel has also created an 80486. It too manipulates data 32 bits at a time, but it includes two components that the 80386 does not. One is a built-in 8k RAM cache that works similarly to an external RAM cache (see "How a RAM Cache Works") to ensure that the processor is not forced to wait for the data it needs to do its work. The other component is a built-in math coprocessor. The *coprocessor* is a set of instructions streamlined for handling complex math.

6 The Protection Test Unit, which acts as a traffic cop for the Execution Unit, makes sure that the operations performed by the Execution Unit are legal—that they don't modify locations in memory or access peripherals that they shouldn't. In this case, the Protection Test Unit verifies that the Control Unit can access the address of the first number and forwards it to the Segment and Paging units, where the virtual address is translated into a physical address for use by the Bus Interface Unit.

How a RAM Cache Works

RANDOM ACCESS MEMORY chips are found in all computers, but not all memory chips are created equal. Some are faster than others at refreshing the electrical charges in the capacitors that hold data. The refresh rate—usually described in *nanoseconds*, or billionths of a second—affects how quickly data can move from memory to the microprocessor that manipulates that data.

The faster that RAM chips are, the more expensive they are. To hold down the costs of personal computers, many manufacturers use slower memory chips for the bulk of a PC's memory and a few faster, more expensive RAM chips on the motherboard as an external RAM cache. The cache—usually consisting of 64 to 256 kilobytes of memory—helps move data between the main memory and the processor with the least delay. A RAM cache has the same effect on speeding up memory access that a disk cache has on speeding up disk access.

Without the cache, the processor may sit idle for several clock cycles while it waits for the requested data to be passed to it. A clock cycle is the shortest time during which any operation can happen in a computer. With the cache, however, a computer can keep within arm's reach, so to speak, the data that is mostly likely to be requested by the microprocessor. The data in the faster chips can be provided to the processor with a minimum of delay, sometimes with no delay at all.

Two factors control the effectiveness of a RAM cache. One is the speed of the chips used in the cache—the faster the better. The other factor is the algorithm the cache uses to determine which extra data to store in the cache. The better the algorithm is at guessing which data will be requested next, the more often the cache will come up with a *hit* (the term used to describe each time the processor asks for data and the cache can supply it from the faster chips rather than having to go to slower main RAM).

As new data is requested by your software, the cache replaces the data that has been in the high-speed chips the longest with the new data and other data from surrounding memory addresses. This follows the FIFO rule (first in, first out), which works on the principle that the data that's been lying around unused the longest is the least likely to be requested by the software in the future.

RAM Cache

1 Your software, working through the central processing unit (CPU), requests data or another portion of the software's code to be used by the CPU.

2 The RAM cache, which is built in as part of your PC's main circuitry, intercepts the request as it is on its way to random access memory. The cache fetches the data from RAM and delivers it to the CPU. The first time data is fetched may take several clock cycles during which the CPU can't do any other effective work.

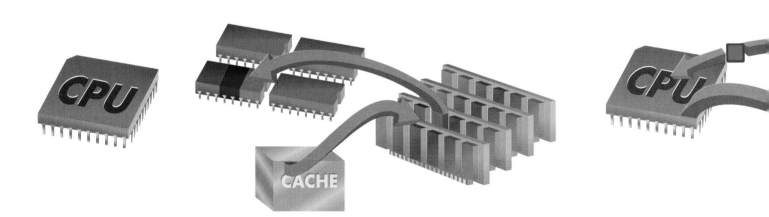

4 As soon as the cache detects that the CPU is idle, it fetches data or program code from memory addresses adjacent to the addresses for the data the software requested originally. The cache stores this data in the high-speed memory chips.

5 The next time the software asks for data to be sent to the CPU, the cache checks to see if that data is already stored in the high-speed memory chips. If it is, the cache can send it directly to the CPU without having to access the slower main memory chips. The CPU spends less time idling and more time working.

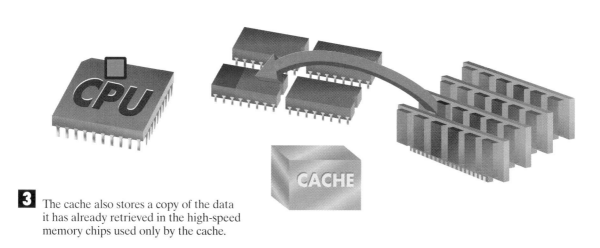

3 The cache also stores a copy of the data it has already retrieved in the high-speed memory chips used only by the cache.

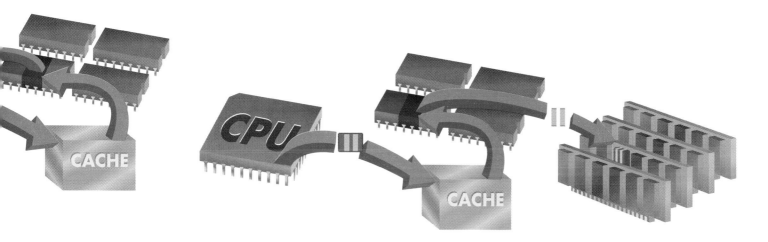

6 When the CPU wants to change something already in memory, the cache first determines if the data to be changed is being held in the high-speed memory chips. If it is, the cache compares the held data with the changes and sends data only to those memory addresses in main RAM that contain data different from the data stored in the high-speed chips. This is faster than changing the entire block of data.

NOTE In addition to the RAM caches found on many PCs based on Intel's 80386 and 80486 DX and SX microprocessors, the 486DX processor contains its own 8k cache within the chip itself. The internal cache works similarly to the way that the external RAM cache works to speed up data movements even more.

DATA STORAGE

3

CONTENTS

S INTELLIGENT AND SWIFT as a computer's memory may be, RAM has one
fatal flaw. It is a will-o'-the wisp. With a few exceptions, all memory chips lose the
information stored in them once you turn off the computer. All the work you've put into
figuring out next year's budget, creating account billings, or writing the great American sit-
com will vanish if the electricity constantly stoking the RAM chips' transistors falters for
even a fraction of a second.

Fortunately, there are several ways to provide permanent storage for a computer's
programs and the work they generate—storage that stays intact even when the power is
turned off. The most common form of permanent storage is magnetic disks—both the
floppy and hard variety. Magnetic storage is also used in the form of tape drives—a method
of permanent storage that's been around almost as long as the first computers. Gaining
popularity are new devices that use lasers to store or retrieve data. And recently, computer
manufacturers have made strides toward creating nonvolatile memory chips that, unlike
their more common RAM chip cousins, don't lose their contents when you turn off your
PC because they have their own built-in power supplies. All of these methods of permanently storing data have their advantages and disadvantages.

Floppy disks are universal, portable, and inexpensive but lack both large capacity
and speed. Hard disks are probably the best all-around storage medium. They store and
retrieve data quickly, have the capacity to save several volumes of data, and are inexpensive on a cost-per-megabyte basis. But hard disks are generally not portable except for
newer versions available at higher cost. Tape drives provide virtually endless off-line storage at low cost, but they are too slow to use as anything other than a backup medium.

Some of the newer forms of storage serve PC users who need to store enormous
quantities of data. CD-ROM drives can pack up to 500 megabytes of data on a disk
identical to the laser compact disks that play music, and CD-ROM disks are cheap to
produce. But they are read-only devices, which means that you can only use the data
that was stored on them when they were created; you can't use compact disks to store

your own data. Magneto-optical drives, like CD-ROMs, use lasers to read data but have the advantage that they can also write data. They are fast, portable, and have generous storage capacities, but only recently has their cost dropped low enough to make them common.

Two types of memory chips retain their information once a computer is turned off. EPROMs (for Erasable Programmable Read-Only Memory) are found in nearly every personal computer. They are the chips that supply boot-up information to the PC. But they are slow, and their data can be changed only by exposing them first to ultraviolet light. Flash RAM chips, which combine the writability and much of the speed of conventional RAM chips with the ability to retain data when the main power source is turned off, promise to be in common use in the future and may turn out to be the ideal permanent storage medium. But for now, they are too expensive to completely replace hard disks.

Despite the different technologies behind these methods of storage, they all have in common a similar notation for recording data and a similar system for filing that information so that it can be found again. Permanent data storage is similar in concept to paper filing systems. Paper files may be handwritten or typed, but they are all in the same language. And just as paper files thrown willy-nilly into file cabinets would be impossible to retrieve easily and quickly, electronic files to be retrieved must be stored, too, in an orderly and sensible system and in a common language.

In this part of the book, we'll look at how various forms of permanent storage solve the task of saving data so that it can easily be found again, and how different storage devices write and retrieve that data.

How Disk Storage Works

DISKS ARE THE most common form of permanent data storage. Their capacities may range from a few hundred kilobytes to several gigabytes, but they all have some elements in common. For one, the way that a drive's mechanism creates the 1s and 0s that make up the binary language of computers may differ, but the goal is to alter microscopically small areas of the disk surface so some of the areas represent 0s and others represent 1s. The disk has no other characters with which it records a great novel or this week's grocery list.

Another common element is the scheme that determines how the data on the disk is organized. The computer's operating system, which on most personal computers is MS-DOS, determines the scheme. The operating system controls so many of a PC's operations that many PC users forget that *DOS* stands for *Disk Operating System* and that, originally, its primary function was to control disk drives.

Before any information can be stored on a magnetic disk, the disk must first be formatted. Formatting creates a road map that allows the drive to store and find data in an orderly manner. The road map consists of magnetic codes that are embedded in the film to divide the surfaces of the disk into *sectors* (pie slices) and *tracks* (concentric circles). These divisions organize the disk so that data can be recorded in a logical manner and accessed quickly by the read/write heads that move back and forth over the disk as it spins. The number of sectors and tracks that fit on a disk determines the disk capacity.

After a disk is formatted, writing or reading even the simplest file is a complicated process that involves your software, DOS, the PC's BIOS (Basic Input/Output System), and the mechanism of the disk drive itself. The operating system has to have some way of finding any file on the disk. Because a file can be scattered among many separate sections, there has to be a way to keep track of all those sections. And there has to be a method to erase a file so that the space it takes up is free to hold other files.

Writing and Reading Bits on a Disk

1 Before any data is written to a disk, iron particles are scattered in a random pattern within a magnetic film that coats the surface of the disk, which is similar to the surface of audio and video tapes. To organize the particles into data, electricity pulses through a coil of wire wrapped around an iron core in the drive mechanism's read/write head; the head is suspended over the disk's surface. The electricity turns the core into an electromagnet that can move the molecules in the coating, much like a child uses a magnet to play with iron filings.

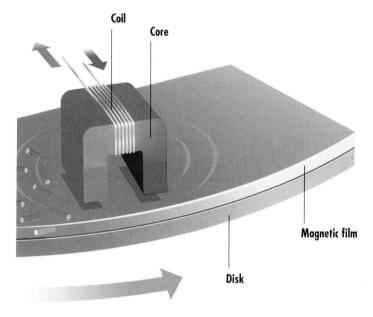

Coil

Core

Magnetic film

Disk

2 The coil induces a magnetic field in the core as it passes over the disk. The field, in turn, magnetizes the iron molecules in the disk coating and forces the molecules to align with their positive poles pointing toward the negative pole of the read/write head, and their negative poles pointing to the head's positive pole. The positive and negative poles are represented here as red and blue, respectively.

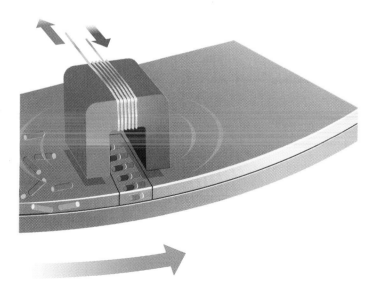

3 After the head creates one magnetic band on the revolving disk, a second band is created next to it. Together, the two bands represent the smallest discrete element of data that a computer can handle—a bit. If the bit is to represent a binary 1, after creating the first band, the current in the coil reverses so that the magnetic poles of the core are swapped and the molecules in the second band are aligned in the opposite direction. If the bit is a binary 0, the molecules in both bands are aligned in the same direction.

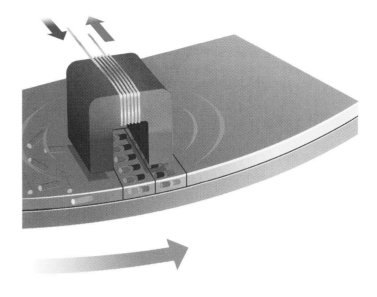

4 When a second bit is stored, the polarity of its first band is always the opposite of the band preceding it to indicate that it's a new bit. Even the slowest drive takes only a fraction of a second to create each band. The stored bits in the illustration below represent the binary number 1011, which is 11 in decimal numbers.

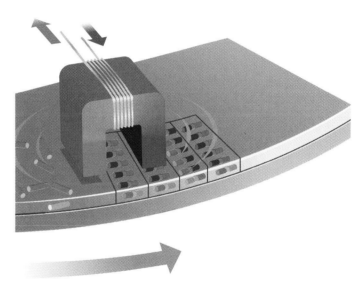

5 To read the data, no current is sent to the read/write head as it passes over the disk. Instead, the magnetic reverse of the writing process happens. The banks of polarized molecules in the disk's coating are themselves tiny magnets that create a magnetic field through which the read/write head passes. The movement of the head through the magnetic field generates an electrical current that travels in one direction or the other through the wires leading from the head. The direction the current flows depends on the polarities of the bands. By sensing the directions in which the current is moving, the computer can tell if the read/write head is passing over a 1 or a 0.

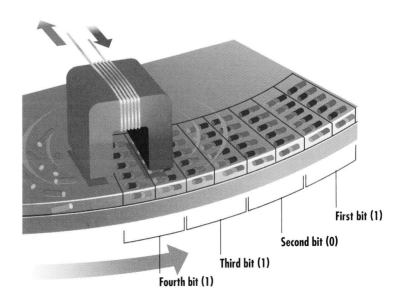

First bit (1)

Second bit (0)

Third bit (1)

Fourth bit (1)

Formatting a Disk

1 The first task a drive must do is to format any disk that is used with it. It does this by writing onto the surface of the disk a pattern of 1s and 0s—like magnetic signposts. The pattern divides the disk radially into sectors and concentric circles. As the read/write head moves back and forth over the spinning disks, it reads these magnetic signposts to determine where it is in relation to the data on the disk's surface.

2 The combination of two or more sectors on a single track makes up a *cluster* or *block*. The number of bytes in a cluster may vary according to the version of DOS used to format the disk and the disk's size. A cluster is the minimum unit DOS uses to store information. Even if a file has a size of only 1 byte, an entire 256–byte cluster may be used to hold the file. The number of sectors and tracks and, therefore, the number of clusters that a drive can create on a disk's surface determine the capacity of the disk.

3 The drive creates a special file located in the disk's sector 0. (In the computer world, numbering often begins with 0 instead of 1.) This file is the file allocation table, or FAT. The FAT is where DOS stores the information about the disk's directory structure and what clusters are used to store which files. In newer versions of DOS, an identical copy of the FAT is kept in another location in case the data in the first FAT becomes corrupted. Ordinarily, you will never see the contents of either FAT.

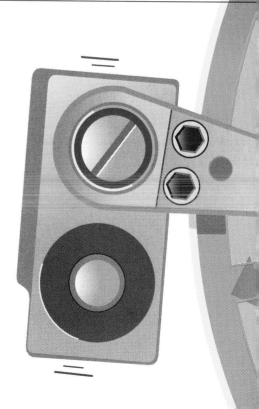

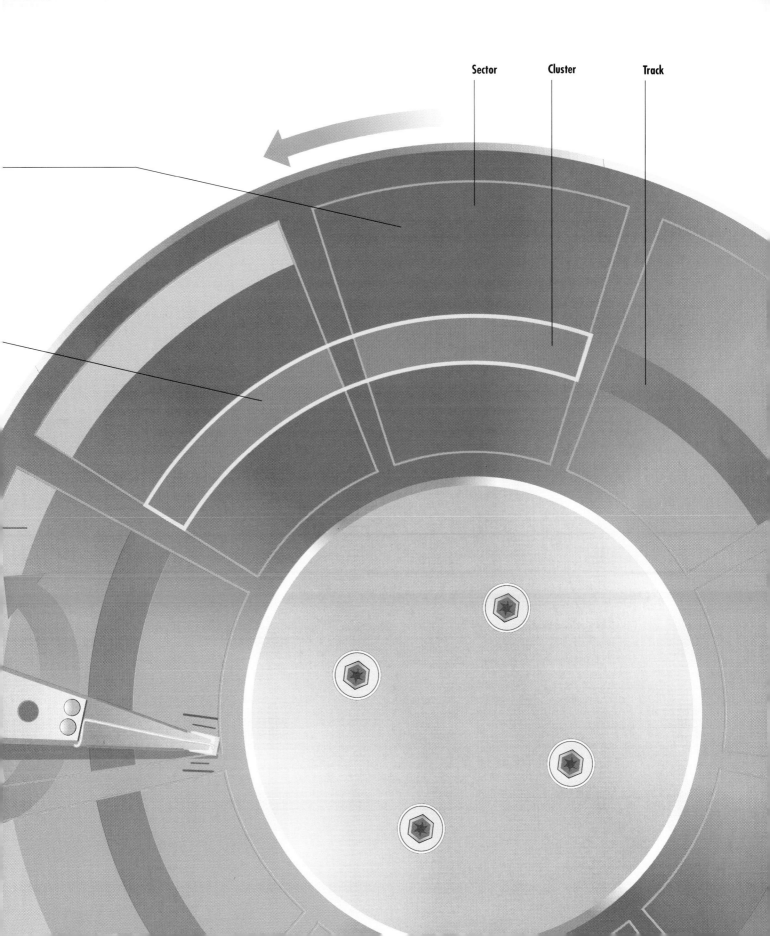

Sector Cluster Track

Writing a File to Disk

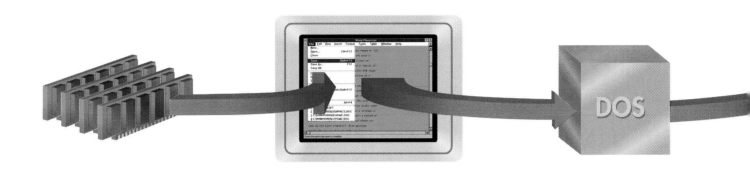

1 When you use the commands or mouse clicks that save a file in your software, the program you're using sends a command to DOS, asking the operating system to carry out the steps needed to save the file to disk. For this example, we'll assume you're using a word processor to save a file named LETTER.TXT.

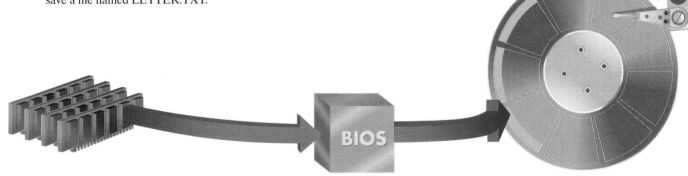

5 The BIOS frees the software from the details of saving the file. It retrieves the data that will make up LETTER.TXT from where the word processor is using it in RAM. At the same time, it issues the instructions to the disk-drive controller to save the data that the BIOS is sending it, beginning at sectors 2 through 5 on track 1.

File Allocation Table

File	Cluster
LWKSHT.WK1	1
REPORT.JAN	2
AVAILABLE	3
BUDGET.WK1	4

Cluster Address

Cluster	Track	Sector
3	1	2,3,4,5

3 DOS also checks the FAT for the number of a cluster where DOS can save the file without overwriting any other data that's already been saved. Here, the FAT tells DOS that cluster 3 is free to receive data.

4 From the FAT, DOS also determines that the location of cluster 3 comprises sectors 2, 3, 4, and 5 on track 1. DOS conveys this information to the PC's BIOS.

DATABASE
WP

LETTER.TXT
MEMO.TXT
REPORT.TXT

2 DOS modifies the directory structure stored in the FAT to indicate that a file named LETTER.TXT will be stored in the current directory (or in another directory if you provide a different directory path).

6 If the file is larger than the number of bytes contained in a single cluster, DOS asks the FAT for the location of another cluster to which it may continue saving the file. The clusters need not be adjacent to each other on the disk. The FAT maintains a record of the chain of clusters over which the file is spread. The process repeats itself until DOS encounters a special code called an end-of-file marker.

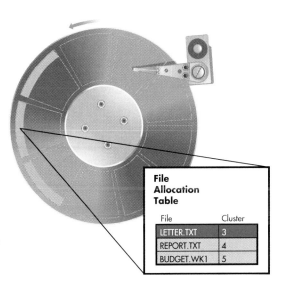

File Allocation Table

File	Cluster
LETTER.TXT	3
REPORT.TXT	4
BUDGET.WK1	5

7 Finally, DOS tells the FAT to mark the clusters that contain LETTER.TXT so that later, DOS will know the clusters are already being used.

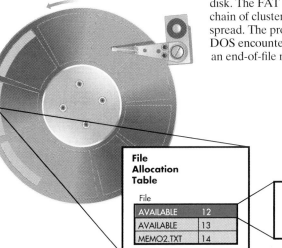

File Allocation Table

File	
AVAILABLE	12
AVAILABLE	13
MEMO2.TXT	14

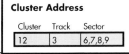

Cluster Address

Cluster	Track	Sector
12	3	6,7,8,9

Reading a File from a Disk

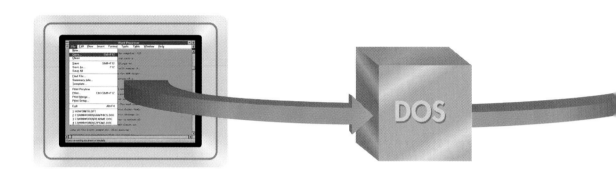

1 When you use your software's commands or menu functions to retrieve a file named LETTER.TXT, your software passes along the command and the name of the file to DOS.

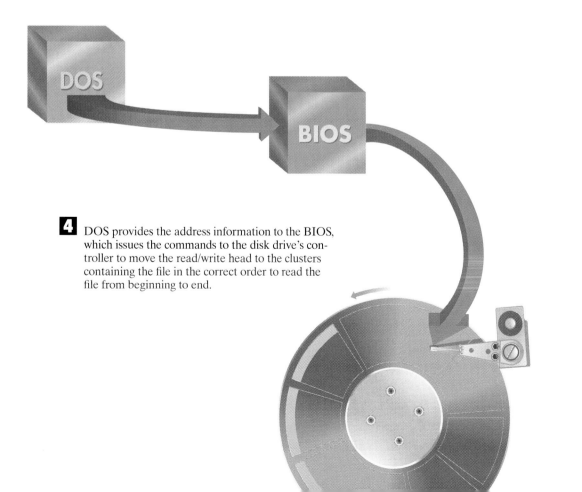

4 DOS provides the address information to the BIOS, which issues the commands to the disk drive's controller to move the read/write head to the clusters containing the file in the correct order to read the file from beginning to end.

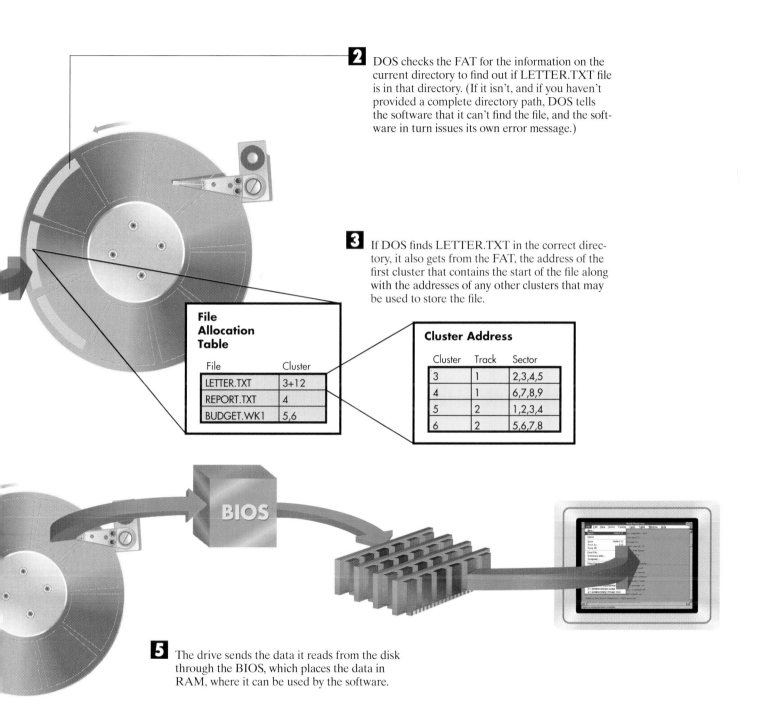

2 DOS checks the FAT for the information on the current directory to find out if LETTER.TXT file is in that directory. (If it isn't, and if you haven't provided a complete directory path, DOS tells the software that it can't find the file, and the software in turn issues its own error message.)

3 If DOS finds LETTER.TXT in the correct directory, it also gets from the FAT, the address of the first cluster that contains the start of the file along with the addresses of any other clusters that may be used to store the file.

File Allocation Table

File	Cluster
LETTER.TXT	3+12
REPORT.TXT	4
BUDGET.WK1	5,6

Cluster Address

Cluster	Track	Sector
3	1	2,3,4,5
4	1	6,7,8,9
5	2	1,2,3,4
6	2	5,6,7,8

5 The drive sends the data it reads from the disk through the BIOS, which places the data in RAM, where it can be used by the software.

NOTE When you tell your software or DOS to delete a file, the data that makes up the file is not actually erased from the disk. Instead, DOS rewrites the information in the FAT about the file's clusters to indicate that those clusters may be reused by other files. Because the data remains on disk until the clusters are reused, you can often restore a file that you've accidentally erased.

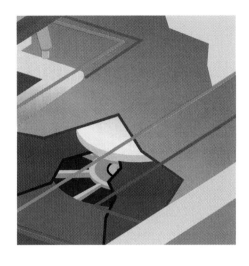

How a Floppy Drive Works

AMID SUPERFAST, SUPERBIG hard drives, magneto-optical drives, CD-ROM drives, and all the other newest high-tech marvels, it's hard to get excited about the common floppy drive. It's slow and doesn't store very much compared to any other type of drive.

But for all its deficiencies, the floppy drive is an underappreciated wonder. An entire bookful of information can be contained on a disk that you can slip into your pocket or a briefcase. Floppy drives are ubiquitous, making them a sure and convenient way to get data from one PC to another. No communication lines, networks, or infrared links are needed; just pull the floppy out of one machine and slip it into another.

With his NeXT computer, Steve Jobs tried to eliminate the floppy entirely and promote the magneto-optical drive as the ideal method of distributing commercial software. The idea had a note of technological idealism to it, but no one thought very highly of it. For all its commoner heritage, the floppy is dependable and respectable. It will be with us in some form for a long time to come.

Although smaller, faster, and more capacious floppy drives are becoming standard components of all new computers, it's hard to be without the old 5.25-inch floppy drive. It's the 78-rpm phonograph record of the computer world. Long after smaller records that played more music with greater fidelity were available, phonograph companies continued to produce turntables with 78-rpm settings just because many music lovers had so much invested in 78s. And 5.25-inch drives are a similar necessity. We've got too much data stored on them and they're too often needed to exchange data with users who don't have newer drives.

When the 5.25-inch drive is supplanted, its heir will not be the magneto-optical drive that Jobs envisioned, but some variation of the 3.5-inch drive. With capacities today ranging from 700 kilobytes to 2.88 megabytes, the smaller disks hold more data than their bigger cousins. Their protective cases mean that we can be downright careless about how we handle them. They are dramatically less expensive than similarly sized removable hard drives—so cheap that their cost is not a factor. And they are already the standard for portable computing.

At some point we may have cheap, portable storage using flash memory chips in a form no larger than a credit card. But for many years to come, you can be sure that some sort of floppy drive will be standard equipment on all personal computers.

3.5-inch Floppy Drive

1 When a 3.5-inch floppy disk is inserted into the drive, it presses against a system of levers. One lever opens the shutter to expose the *cookie*—the mylar disk coated on either side with a magnetic material that can record data.

7 When the heads are in the correct position, electrical impulses create a magnetic field in one of the heads to write data to either the top or bottom surface of the disk. When the heads are reading data, they react to magnetic fields generated by the metallic particles on the disk.

6 A stepper motor—which can turn a specific amount in either direction according to signals from the circuit board—moves a second shaft that has a spiral groove cut into it. An arm attached to the read/write heads rests inside the shaft's groove. As the shaft turns, the arm moves back and forth, positioning the read/write heads over the disk.

5 A motor located beneath the disk spins a shaft that engages a notch on the hub of the disk, causing the disk to spin.

2 Other levers and gears move two read/write heads until they almost touch the cookie on either side. The heads, which are tiny electromagnets, use magnetic pulses to change the polarity of metallic particles embedded in the disk's coating.

3 The drive's circuit board receives signals, including data and instructions for writing that data to disk, from the floppy drive's controller board. The circuit board translates the instructions into signals that control the movement of the disk and the read/write heads.

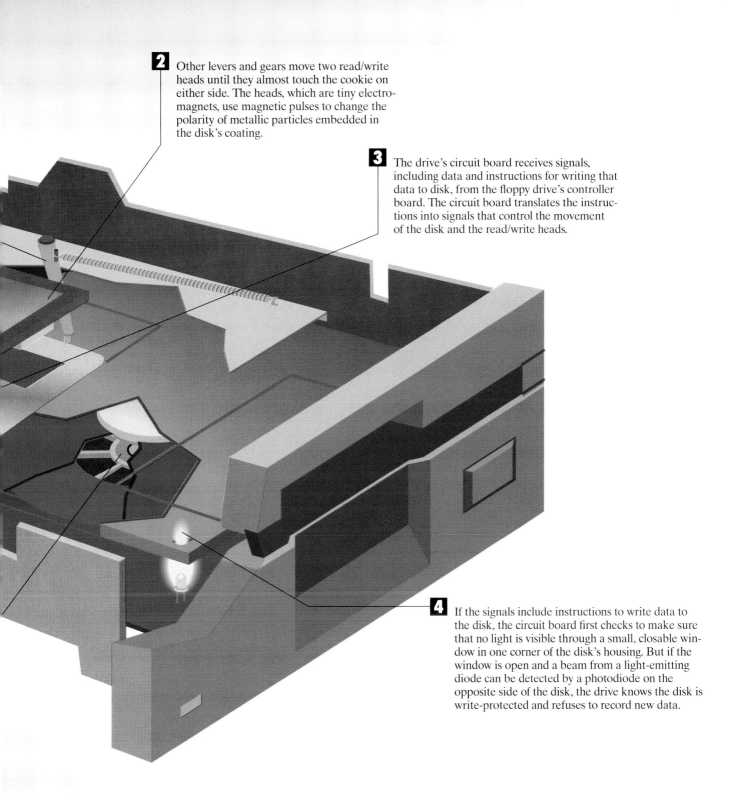

4 If the signals include instructions to write data to the disk, the circuit board first checks to make sure that no light is visible through a small, closable window in one corner of the disk's housing. But if the window is open and a beam from a light-emitting diode can be detected by a photodiode on the opposite side of the disk, the drive knows the disk is write-protected and refuses to record new data.

NOTE Despite its different size and casing, the 5.25-inch floppy disk is simply a bigger, slower, less complicated version of the 3.5-inch disk. It has no door to open, but the notch on its side is checked for write protection, and the read/write heads of the drive work identically to those of the smaller drive.

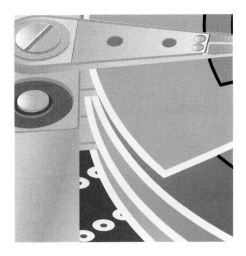

How a Hard Drive Works

A HARD DRIVE IS the workaholic of a PC system. The platters on which data is stored spin at a breakneck speed as long as the computer is turned on (except for portable PCs that periodically turn off the drive's spin to conserve battery life). Each access of the hard drive to read or write a file results in a furious flurry of movement—which must be performed with microscopic precision—by the read/write heads. So exacting are the tolerances in a hard drive—the gaps between the heads and the platters aren't big enough to admit a human hair—that it's a wonder the drive can perform its work at all without constant disasters. Instead, it keeps on plugging away as the repository of perhaps years of work—with surprisingly few failures.

The capacity, form, and performance of hard drives have changed dramatically since the introduction of the first IBM XT with a hard drive in the early 1980s. Back then, a capacity of 10 megabytes was considered generous. The hard drive was 3 to 4 inches thick and filled a 5.25-inch drive bay. An access time of 87 milliseconds was warp speed compared to the access times of floppy drives. A decade later, hard drives that hold 200 megabytes in a size smaller than that of a 3.5-inch floppy drive and with access speeds of 18 milliseconds are inexpensive and commonplace. The latest hard drives pack 20 megabytes or more on removable disks no larger than a matchbox. In the future, the size of drives will continue to decrease at the same time that their capacities increase.

One thing about hard drives will probably stay the same. Unlike other PC components that obey the commands of software without complaint, the hard drive chatters and groans as it goes about its job. Those noises are reminders that the hard drive is one of the few components of a personal computer that is mechanical as well as electronic. The drive's mechanical components, in more ways than one, make it where the action is.

Hard-Disk Drive

3 A spindle connected to an electrical motor spins as many as eight magnetically coated platters at several thousand rotations per minute. The number of platters and the composition of the magnetic material coating them determine the capacity of the drive. Today's platters, typically, are coated with an alloy about 3 millionths of an inch thick.

2 On the bottom of the drive, a printed circuit board, also known as a logic board, receives commands from the drive's controller, which in turn is controlled by the operating system. The logic board translates those commands into voltage fluctuations that force the head actuator to move the read/write heads across the platters' surfaces. The board also makes sure that the spindle turning the platters is revolving at a constant speed, and the board tells the drive heads when to read and when to write to the disk. On an IDE (Integrated Drive Electronics) disk, the disk controller is part of the logic board.

1 A sealed metal housing protects the internal components from dust particles that could block the narrow gap between the read/write heads and the platters and cause the drive to crash by plowing a furrow in a platter's magnetic coating.

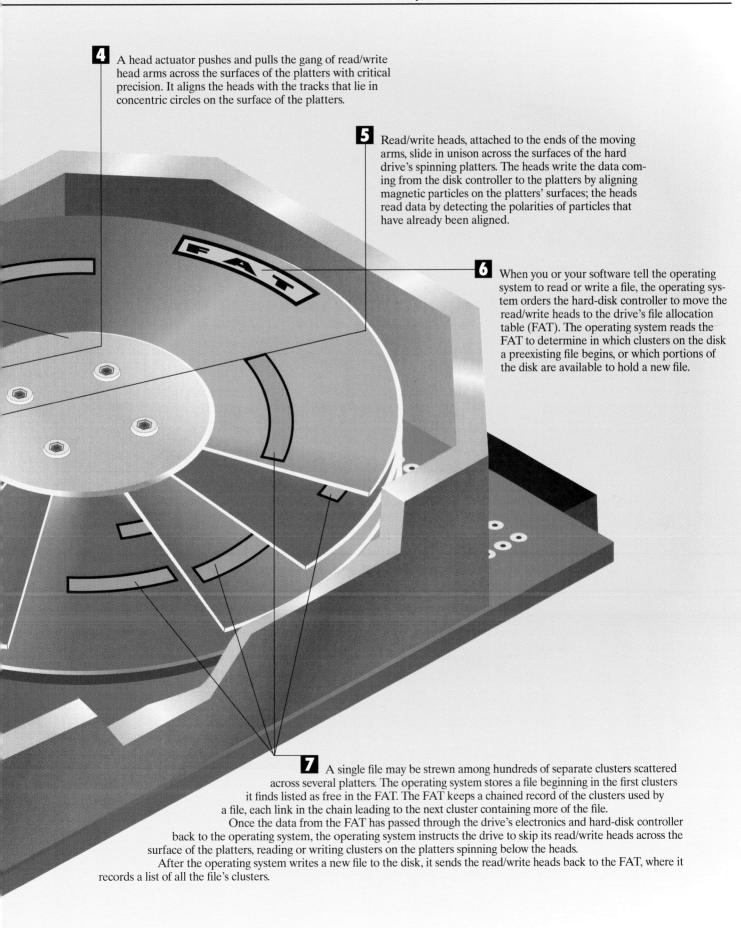

4 A head actuator pushes and pulls the gang of read/write head arms across the surfaces of the platters with critical precision. It aligns the heads with the tracks that lie in concentric circles on the surface of the platters.

5 Read/write heads, attached to the ends of the moving arms, slide in unison across the surfaces of the hard drive's spinning platters. The heads write the data coming from the disk controller to the platters by aligning magnetic particles on the platters' surfaces; the heads read data by detecting the polarities of particles that have already been aligned.

6 When you or your software tell the operating system to read or write a file, the operating system orders the hard-disk controller to move the read/write heads to the drive's file allocation table (FAT). The operating system reads the FAT to determine in which clusters on the disk a preexisting file begins, or which portions of the disk are available to hold a new file.

7 A single file may be strewn among hundreds of separate clusters scattered across several platters. The operating system stores a file beginning in the first clusters it finds listed as free in the FAT. The FAT keeps a chained record of the clusters used by a file, each link in the chain leading to the next cluster containing more of the file.

Once the data from the FAT has passed through the drive's electronics and hard-disk controller back to the operating system, the operating system instructs the drive to skip its read/write heads across the surface of the platters, reading or writing clusters on the platters spinning below the heads.

After the operating system writes a new file to the disk, it sends the read/write heads back to the FAT, where it records a list of all the file's clusters.

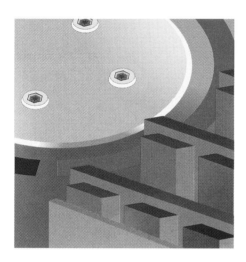

How a Disk Cache Works

THE SLOWEST PART of any computer is its disk drives. The drives and your keyboard are the only major portions of your personal computer that contain moving parts. The rest of your PC merely has to shuttle electrons here and there. But mechanical parts move in the real world of mass and inertia. No matter how fast your hard drive may be, its mechanical parts make it a sluggard compared to other components that move data at the speed of electricity.

There are ways to minimize a drive's inherent slowness. Some drives are faster than others. You can make sure that the files on a disk are *defragmented*—that is, the clusters that make up the files are next to each other so the read/write heads don't have to travel all over the disk to retrieve the separate parts of the file. And you can avoid using a physical drive by using a RAM drive, which is part of your PC's memory configured to fool the PC into thinking it's a real disk drive.

Despite these tricks, however, it's impossible to eliminate disk accesses completely. Reading programs and data files from disk is essential to any meaningful computing. The most effective and universal way to compensate for the slowness of disk drives is to use a disk cache. Essentially a disk cache speeds up your computer's operations by keeping in RAM the data your applications are mostly likely to request from the drive.

The concept behind a disk cache is similar to that of a RAM cache. (See "How a RAM Cache Works.") But because the difference in speed between a disk drive and any RAM chips is so much greater than the difference between a slow RAM chip and a fast RAM chip, a disk cache provides results that are much more dramatic than those of a RAM cache. There are several disk-cache programs for sale, and one comes with MS-DOS. Some are better than others, but even the least effective disk cache is an astonishing improvement over no cache at all.

More advanced disk controllers come with circuitry for caching drives and their own RAM so that the cache doesn't use memory that your programs could use. But you can achieve similar results by loading an inexpensive memory-resident cache program that uses your main system memory to cache your drives.

Disk Cache

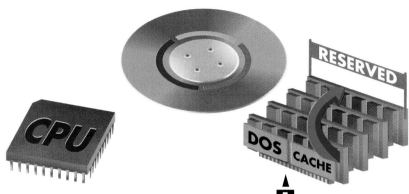

1 When you load a software disk cache, the memory-resident program reserves a section of conventional, expanded, or extended memory for its exclusive use. The amount used by the cache can be anything from a few kilobytes to several megabytes of RAM; generally, the more RAM a cache can use, the more effective it is. Some caches reserve a specific amount of memory; others claim all the memory that's available but later release portions of the memory as other programs need it for their own work.

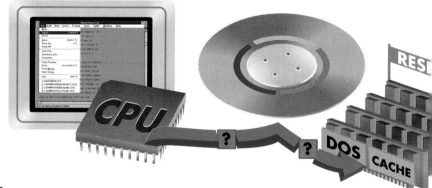

2 The CPU, under the direction of your application software, issues a command to the hard disk for data. The cache intercepts the data request.

3 The cache reads the data from the disk, but in addition to the requested data, it also fetches more data, usually from adjacent clusters on the drive. The cache passes the requested data to the CPU, but stores a copy of it, along with the excess data also fetched, in the RAM it reserved earlier.

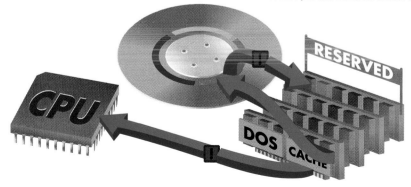

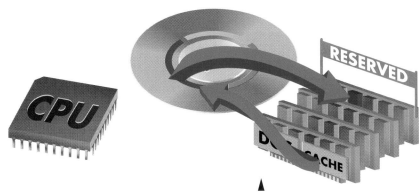

4 During the frequent moments when the CPU is not actively engaged in processing instructions, the cache takes control to read still more data from the drive, which it also stores in RAM, usually from sectors near the files that have already been read. Every cache has a built-in logic that makes intelligent guesses about which clusters are more likely to be requested later by the application. The intelligence of this logic distinguishes one cache's efficiency from another's.

5 Later, when the program requests more data, the cache again intercepts the request and checks to see if the requested data is already stored in RAM. If it is, the cache supplies the data directly to the CPU without having to access the disk. But if the data is not there, the cache repeats the earlier process, retrieving the new data, supplying it to the CPU, and also storing it in RAM along with extra clusters from the disk. As the RAM used by the cache fills up, the cache releases the data that's been in the buffer the longest without being used and replaces it with data gathered during more recent disk accesses.

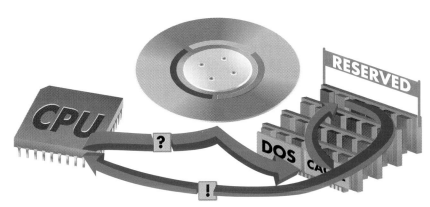

6 When a program issues a command to save data to disk, some caches intercept the data and defer writing it to disk until the CPU is otherwise idle. This speeds up computer operations because the CPU's attention is not divided between writing to disk and other processing.

7 If the file to be written to disk is still held in the area of RAM controlled by the cache, then the cache writes to disk only the clusters that have been changed. Some caches also hold pending writes and perform them in an order that minimizes the movements of the disk drive's read/write heads.

NOTE Caching disk controllers work similarly to software-based caches but don't use any ordinary system memory, either for the logic that controls the cache or for storing cached data. Caching disk controllers generally provide better performance but are more expensive than software caches.

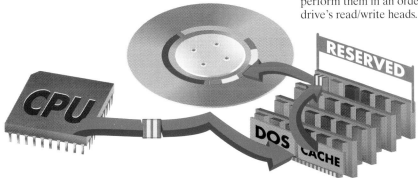

How a CD-ROM Drive Works

A COMPUTER'S CD-ROM drive uses small, plastic-encased disks, like compact music disks, from which data is retrieved using a laser beam. And like a music CD, a computer CD can store vast amounts of information because it uses light to record data in a form that's more tightly packed than the form that the magnetic read/write heads of a conventional drive can manage. And like a music CD, a computer compact disk is a read-only device; you can't use it to store your own data.

The huge capacity and read-only nature of CD-ROM disks, combined with the relatively low cost of the drives, makes the disks the perfect medium for storing massive data that doesn't need frequent updating. You can easily find CD-ROM disks filled with clip art, photographs, encyclopedias, the complete works of Shakespeare, and entire bookshelves of reference literature. CD-ROM drives are also a basic component of multimedia systems, which use video and sound files that are, typically, mammoth. (An added bonus of their multimedia capabilities is that most CD-ROM drives will also let you play ordinary compact music disks.)

Unlike an audio CD player, a CD-ROM drive is nearly devoid of buttons and LCD readouts, except for a button to load and unload a disk and a single light that shows when the disk is being read. The CD-ROM drive is controlled by software in your PC that sends instructions to controller circuitry that's either on the computer's motherboard or on a separate board installed in an expansion slot. Together, the software and circuitry manipulate high-tech components that make conventional drives seem crude in comparison.

CD-ROM Drive

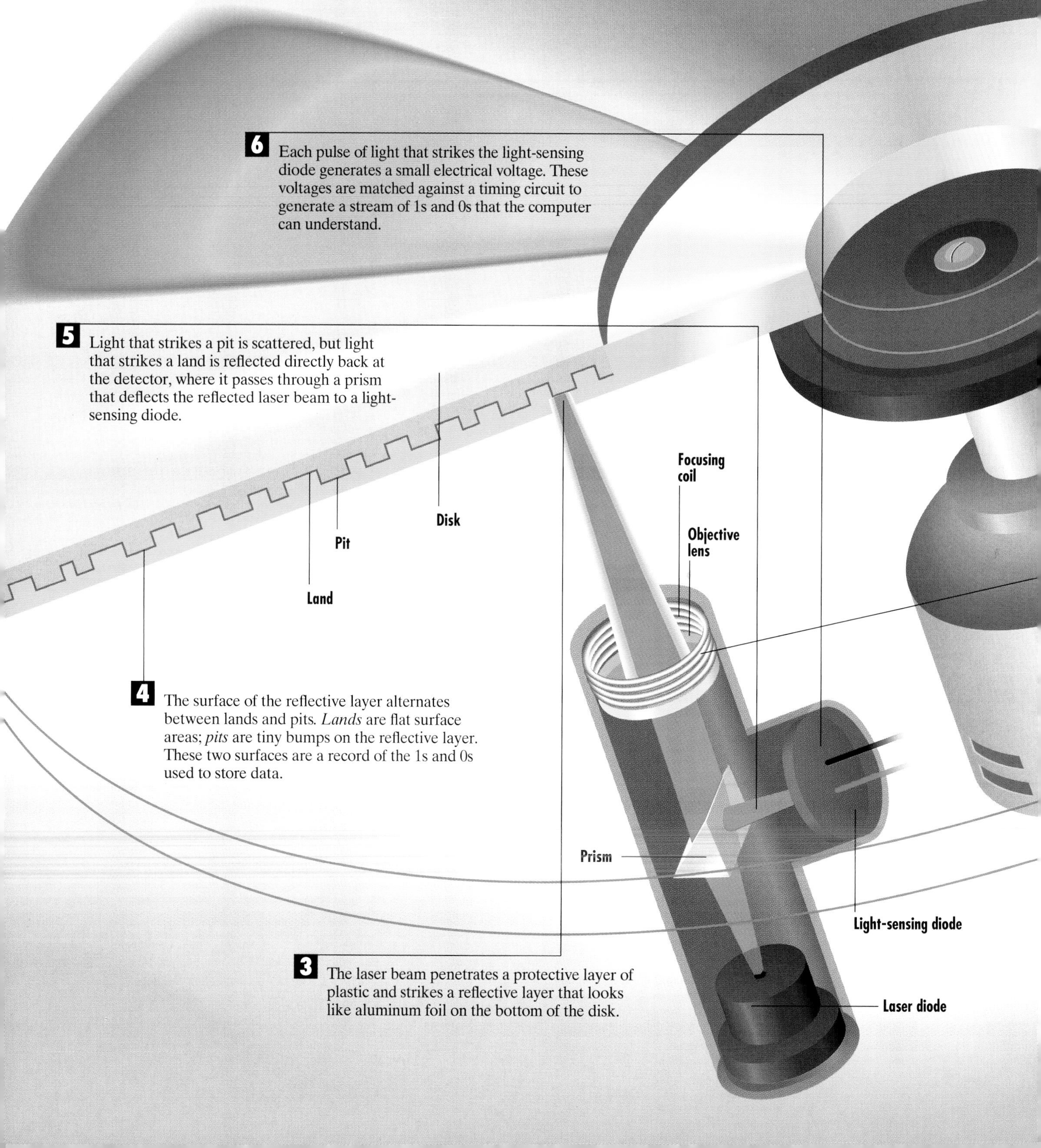

6 Each pulse of light that strikes the light-sensing diode generates a small electrical voltage. These voltages are matched against a timing circuit to generate a stream of 1s and 0s that the computer can understand.

5 Light that strikes a pit is scattered, but light that strikes a land is reflected directly back at the detector, where it passes through a prism that deflects the reflected laser beam to a light-sensing diode.

Disk

Pit

Land

Focusing coil

Objective lens

4 The surface of the reflective layer alternates between lands and pits. *Lands* are flat surface areas; *pits* are tiny bumps on the reflective layer. These two surfaces are a record of the 1s and 0s used to store data.

Prism

Light-sensing diode

3 The laser beam penetrates a protective layer of plastic and strikes a reflective layer that looks like aluminum foil on the bottom of the disk.

Laser diode

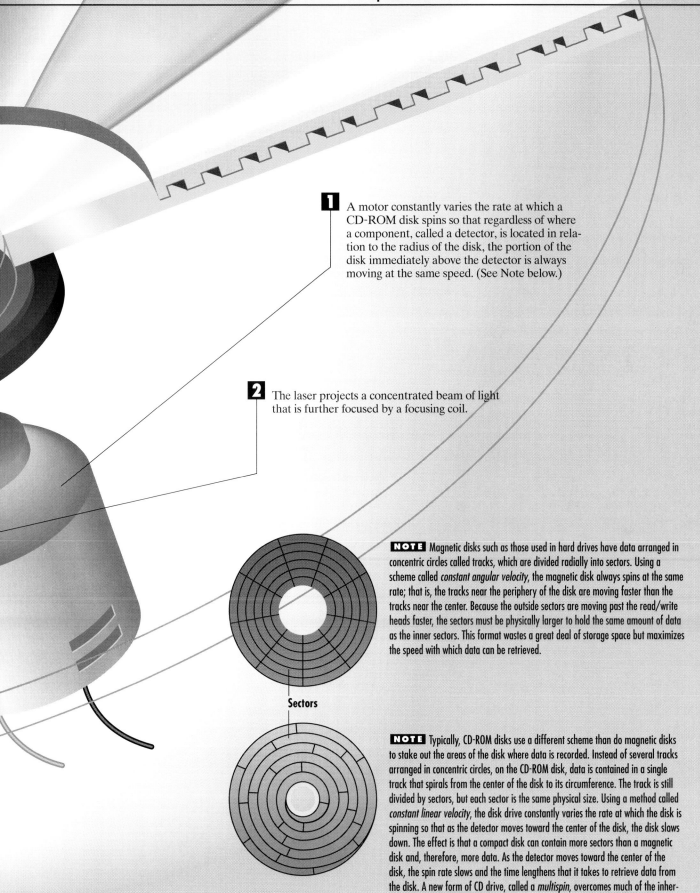

1 A motor constantly varies the rate at which a CD-ROM disk spins so that regardless of where a component, called a detector, is located in relation to the radius of the disk, the portion of the disk immediately above the detector is always moving at the same speed. (See Note below.)

2 The laser projects a concentrated beam of light that is further focused by a focusing coil.

NOTE Magnetic disks such as those used in hard drives have data arranged in concentric circles called tracks, which are divided radially into sectors. Using a scheme called *constant angular velocity*, the magnetic disk always spins at the same rate; that is, the tracks near the periphery of the disk are moving faster than the tracks near the center. Because the outside sectors are moving past the read/write heads faster, the sectors must be physically larger to hold the same amount of data as the inner sectors. This format wastes a great deal of storage space but maximizes the speed with which data can be retrieved.

Sectors

NOTE Typically, CD-ROM disks use a different scheme than do magnetic disks to stake out the areas of the disk where data is recorded. Instead of several tracks arranged in concentric circles, on the CD-ROM disk, data is contained in a single track that spirals from the center of the disk to its circumference. The track is still divided by sectors, but each sector is the same physical size. Using a method called *constant linear velocity*, the disk drive constantly varies the rate at which the disk is spinning so that as the detector moves toward the center of the disk, the disk slows down. The effect is that a compact disk can contain more sectors than a magnetic disk and, therefore, more data. As the detector moves toward the center of the disk, the spin rate slows and the time lengthens that it takes to retrieve data from the disk. A new form of CD drive, called a *multispin*, overcomes much of the inherited slowness of CD drives.

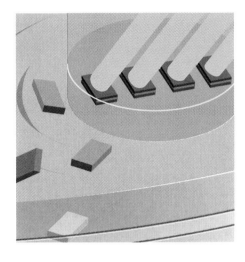

CHAPTER 13

How a Magneto-Optical Drive Works

THE MAGNETIC SIGNALS used by conventional floppy drives and hard disks save data in microscopic strips. And yet on a universal scale, the magnetic signals are crude. In contrast, a beam of light produced by a laser can be narrowed to an area that is much smaller than that affected by even the most sensitive magnetic read/write head. Obviously, if a laser beam could be used to read and write disks, then more data could be packed into the same space.

The first attempts to harness the laser beam as a read/write device resulted in a WORM—from Write Once, Read Many. A WORM could, indeed, pack hundreds of megabytes of data onto a single, removable disk. The problem with a WORM is that once data was written to a disk, it could not be changed or even deleted. An elaborate file-tracking scheme made it possible for a new version of a file to be written to the disk while hiding the original version. The scheme worked all right, but was not an ideal solution. Theoretically, it is possible to fill an entire 500MB WORM disk with only a single 1k file. Today, WORM drives are useful only in situations where you want to keep an unalterable audit trail of transactions.

One solution to the need for removable mass storage that could be erased and altered comes in the form of the magneto-optical (MO) drive, which combines the technology and advantages of both conventional magnetic drives and laser beam-based CD-ROM and WORM drives. The laser used with MO drives lets data be packed so tightly that hundreds of megabytes of information are contained on a single disk that can be moved—like a compact disk—from one machine to another. As with magnetic drives, you can write, change, and delete your own data, avoiding the read-only limitation of CD-ROMs and the write-once limitation of WORMs. In addition, the disks are not affected by magnetic fields at room temperature. And, because an MO's read/write head is farther away from the surface of the disk, crashes are less likely. These one-two technology punches make magneto-optical disks an ideal medium for backup and portable mass storage.

Writing Data to a Magneto-Optical Disk

1 An intense laser beam is focused on the surface of the disk, which is composed of a crystalline metal alloy only a few atoms thick. The alloy, which polarizes light, rides on an aluminum substrate. Both the alloy and the substrate are sandwiched between two sheets of plastic.

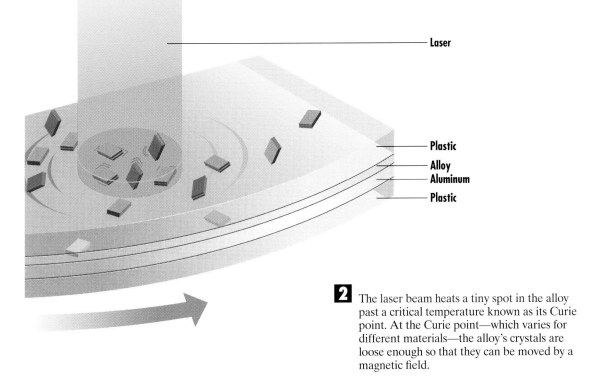

Laser

Plastic
Alloy
Aluminum
Plastic

2 The laser beam heats a tiny spot in the alloy past a critical temperature known as its Curie point. At the Curie point—which varies for different materials—the alloy's crystals are loose enough so that they can be moved by a magnetic field.

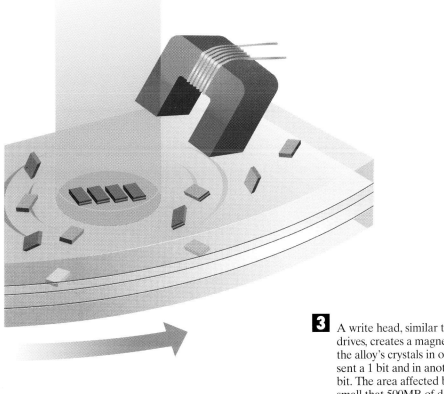

3 A write head, similar to that in conventional drives, creates a magnetic field that realigns the alloy's crystals in one direction to represent a 1 bit and in another, to represent a 0 bit. The area affected by the laser beam is so small that 500MB of data can be stored on a single side of a 5.25-inch disk.

Reading Data from a Magneto-Optical Disk

1 A weaker laser beam is focused along the tracks that contain data written earlier by the more intense laser beam.

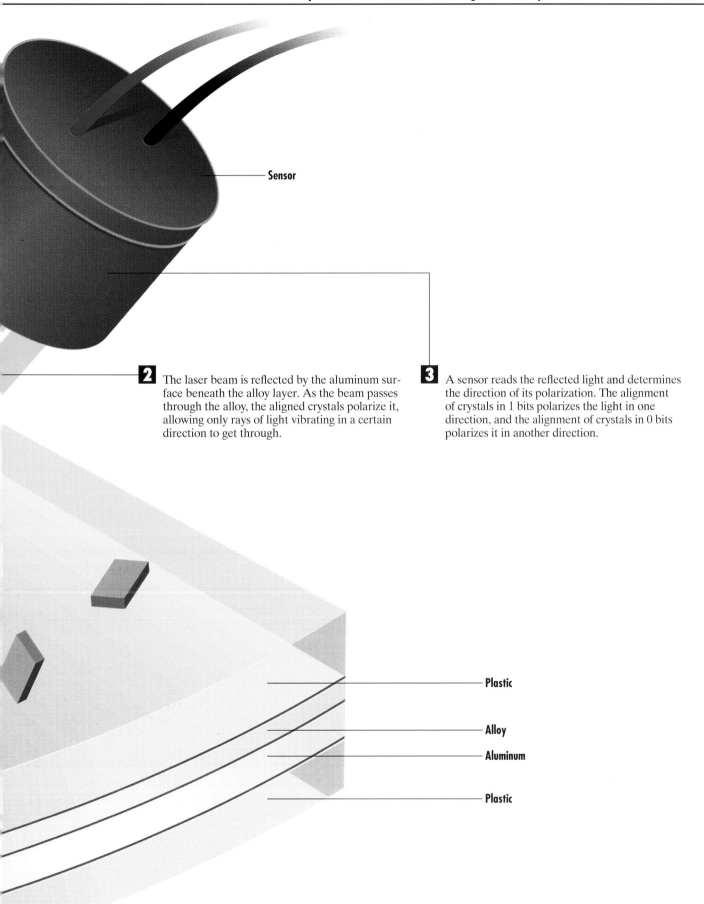

Sensor

2 The laser beam is reflected by the aluminum surface beneath the alloy layer. As the beam passes through the alloy, the aligned crystals polarize it, allowing only rays of light vibrating in a certain direction to get through.

3 A sensor reads the reflected light and determines the direction of its polarization. The alignment of crystals in 1 bits polarizes the light in one direction, and the alignment of crystals in 0 bits polarizes it in another direction.

Plastic

Alloy

Aluminum

Plastic

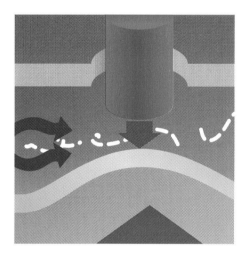

How a Bernoulli Drive Works

AN EIGHTEENTH CENTURY Swiss mathematician, Daniel Bernoulli, was the first person to describe a particular phenomenon of fluid dynamics involving moving water or air. The principle Bernoulli observed is the same one that causes an airplane to lift off the ground.

Bernoulli noticed that the faster air moves, the less pressure it exerts on objects it is flowing past. An airplane's wing is curved on the top so that air moving over the wing has to travel farther than air moving under the wing. But because the air above and below the wing must travel their respective paths in the same amount of time, the air above the wing has to move faster. When the air below presses against the wing with more force than the air above the wing, the plane takes off. You can demonstrate this principle yourself by blowing across the top of a small strip of paper.

The Bernoulli principle inspired an unusual storage device created by Iomega Corporation in the early 1980s. It was unusual because it had the same capacity of hard drives of the time, but the disk could be removed just like a floppy disk. The Bernoulli Box, as it is called, gives unlimited mass storage capacity in a form that's far more convenient than floppy drives.

Competitors have since developed various types of removable hard disks. But few devices besides the Bernoulli Box provide the same improved protection against drive-head crashes.

Bernoulli Drive

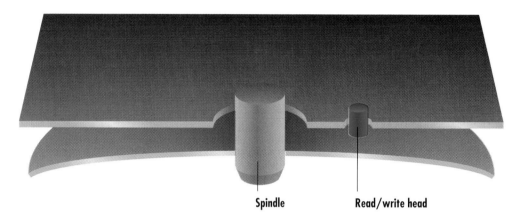

Spindle   **Read/write head**

1 When the flexible material that makes up the disk within a Bernoulli cartridge is at rest, the disk naturally droops down, away from the drive's read/write head.

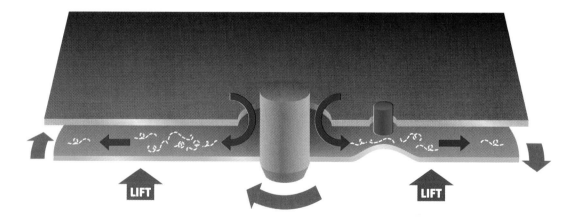

LIFT   LIFT

2 When the drive's spindle begins to spin the disk, the motion pulls air in through an opening in a plate and across the top of the disk. The air below the disk is relatively stable and presses against the bottom of the disk harder than the air moving above the disk presses down on it. The difference in pressure causes the disk to rise toward the plate. The same Bernoulli effect is exaggerated where the read/write head protrudes through the plate, and the disk there is lifted even closer to the head.

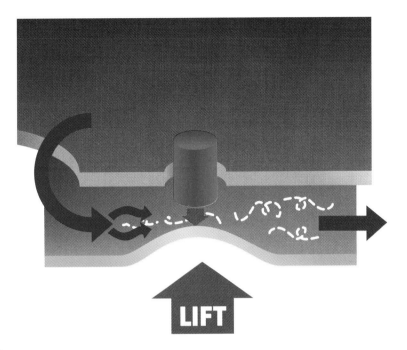

3 The disk does not touch the head because the stationary plate creates an air barrier between the head and the disk. The opposite forces of lift and the air barrier result in the disk stabilizing within 10 millionths of an inch from the read/write head, closer than the distance between a hard disk and its read/write head.

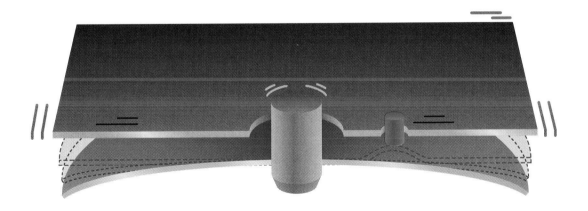

4 In the case of a condition that ordinarily might cause a hard drive to crash—such as a power loss or a jarred drive—the Bernoulli disk, instead, loses some of its lift and the disk falls away from the read/write head, reducing the chance that the disk will touch the head and damage the disk's magnetic film on which data is stored.

How a Tape Backup Drive Works

BACKING UP YOUR hard disk to a tape drive used to be like one of your mother's warnings when you were a child: Take an umbrella with you on cloudy days and always wear a raincoat. Sure, Mom was right once in a while—rain would come down and you would get wet, but it wasn't all that terrible. So what if your hard disk's file allocation table got scrambled and you lost half your files. A few years ago, as long as you'd copied a few essential data files to floppies, recreating a couple of megabytes of programs from their original distribution disks wasn't that much trouble.

Today, however, the implications of a "little" hard-disk disaster have mushroomed. You're more often talking about hard drives that contain not just a few megs of files, but hundreds. A single Windows program may include 20 megabytes of files. And with a complex environment such as Windows, no program exists alone. Each Windows program you install modifies at least one of the .INI files of Windows. Plus, how many tweaks have you made to your system—from arcane parameters to a memory manager's device-driver line in CONFIG.SYS to the Windows color scheme you spent hours perfecting—tweaks you could never hope to remember?

At the same time that it becomes more critical than ever to back up hard drives, disk sizes of over 200 megabytes make the idea of backing up to floppy disks even more abhorrent. Enter the new breed of less expensive, more capacious tape backup drives. Prices well under $500 make them affordable even for home systems. And the ability to copy a gigabyte or more to a single tape makes them simple to use for even the biggest hard drives.

Here's the workings inside two of the most popular types of tape backups: quarter-inch cartridge (QIC) and digital audio tape (DAT).

Quarter-inch Cartridge (QIC) Backup Drive

1 When you use the software for a quarter-inch cartridge drive to issue a backup command, the program reads your hard disk's file allocation table to locate the files you've told it to back up. The software writes the directory information to a 32k buffer in your PC's RAM. It then copies the files into the same buffer. Each file is prefaced with header information that identifies the file and its location on the hard drive's directory tree.

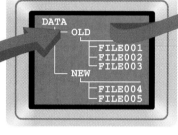

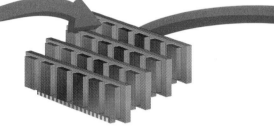

6 As either end of the tape approaches the drive head, holes punched in the tape signal the drive to reverse the direction of the tape and to shift the active area of the recording head up or down to the next track and then continue recording. When all the data has been written to the tape, the backup software updates the tape's directory with the track and segment locations of the files that it's backed up.

5 The format of a QIC tape typically contains 20 to 32 parallel tracks. When the tape reaches either end of a spool, its movement reverses and the flow of data loops back in a spiral fashion to the next outside track. Each track is divided into blocks of 512 or 1,024 bytes, and segments typically contain 32 blocks. Of the blocks in a segment, eight contain error-correction codes. In addition, at the end of each block, the drive computes a *cyclic redundancy check* (CRC) for further error correction and appends it to the block. Most backup software reserves space for a directory of backed-up files at the beginning of track 0 or in a separate directory track.

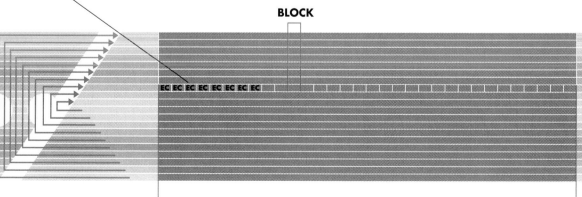

BLOCK

SEGMENT

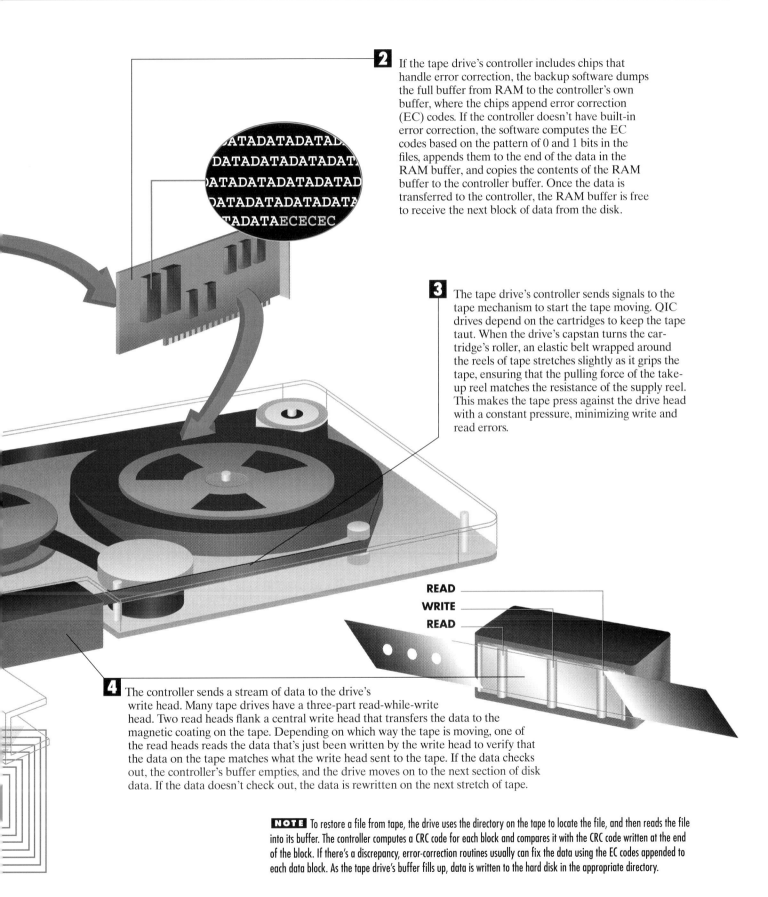

2 If the tape drive's controller includes chips that handle error correction, the backup software dumps the full buffer from RAM to the controller's own buffer, where the chips append error correction (EC) codes. If the controller doesn't have built-in error correction, the software computes the EC codes based on the pattern of 0 and 1 bits in the files, appends them to the end of the data in the RAM buffer, and copies the contents of the RAM buffer to the controller buffer. Once the data is transferred to the controller, the RAM buffer is free to receive the next block of data from the disk.

3 The tape drive's controller sends signals to the tape mechanism to start the tape moving. QIC drives depend on the cartridges to keep the tape taut. When the drive's capstan turns the cartridge's roller, an elastic belt wrapped around the reels of tape stretches slightly as it grips the tape, ensuring that the pulling force of the take-up reel matches the resistance of the supply reel. This makes the tape press against the drive head with a constant pressure, minimizing write and read errors.

READ
WRITE
READ

4 The controller sends a stream of data to the drive's write head. Many tape drives have a three-part read-while-write head. Two read heads flank a central write head that transfers the data to the magnetic coating on the tape. Depending on which way the tape is moving, one of the read heads reads the data that's just been written by the write head to verify that the data on the tape matches what the write head sent to the tape. If the data checks out, the controller's buffer empties, and the drive moves on to the next section of disk data. If the data doesn't check out, the data is rewritten on the next stretch of tape.

NOTE To restore a file from tape, the drive uses the directory on the tape to locate the file, and then reads the file into its buffer. The controller computes a CRC code for each block and compares it with the CRC code written at the end of the block. If there's a discrepancy, error-correction routines usually can fix the data using the EC codes appended to each data block. As the tape drive's buffer fills up, data is written to the hard disk in the appropriate directory.

Digital Audio-Tape (DAT) Backup Drive

1 When you issue a backup command from your software, the program checks your hard-disk's file allocation table to find the files to back up. Then it copies the data, file by file, into the digital audio tape drive's buffer, which usually has room for 512k or 1MB of data. Like a QIC tape drive, the DAT drive performs an algorithm on the data to create error-correction code that it adds to the data in the buffer.

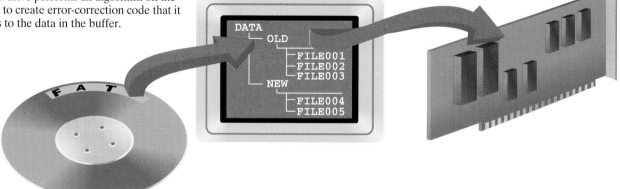

DATA
└ OLD
   ├ FILE001
   ├ FILE002
   ├ FILE003
└ NEW
   ├ FILE004
   ├ FILE005

3 During the time that write head A is in contact with the tape, it writes about 128k of data and error-correction codes from the drive's buffer to a track on the tape. Because the cylinder is tilted, the head encounters one edge of the tape at the beginning of the write head and moves diagonally across the tape until it reaches the other side. This results in a narrow diagonal track about eight times longer than the width of the tape.

4 Read head A reads back and verifies the data in track A, bit by bit, against the data still in the buffer. If the data on the tape checks out, it's flushed from the buffer, and more data is read from the hard disk. If the data in track A contains errors, the data will be rewritten on the next pass.

WRITE HEAD A

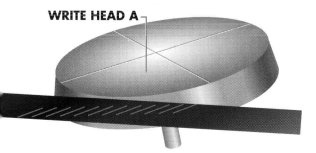

READ HEAD A

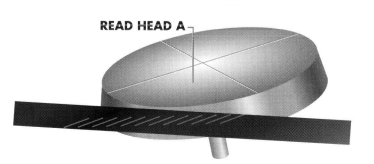

2 The distinctive design of the DAT drive's read/write head is what allows it to back up huge amounts of data onto a small tape cartridge about the size of a matchbox. The mechanism is a rotating cylinder with four heads 90 degrees apart. Two of these heads, write heads A and B, write backup data, and two corresponding read heads verify the data. The cylinder tilts slightly so it rotates at an angle to the tape. The cylinder spins 2,000 times a minute while the tape passes in front of the cylinder in the opposite direction of the cylinder's spin at $1/3$ inch per second.

WRITE HEAD B

READ HEAD B   READ HEAD A

WRITE HEAD A

5 As write head B passes over the tape, it writes data in a track at a 40-degree angle to track A, making a crisscross pattern that overlaps track A. The overlapping data packs more information per inch of tape; it isn't misread later because the magnetic bits written by the two write heads have different polarities, and the different read heads read data only from properly aligned tracks.

6 Read head B and write head B go through the same steps, alternating with the A heads until all the data is backed up. Then the drive rewinds the tape and writes a directory of stored files either in a special partition at the front of the tape or in a file on the hard disk.

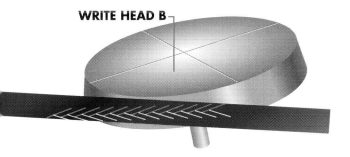

WRITE HEAD B

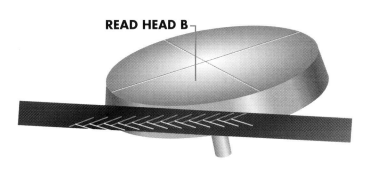

READ HEAD B

NOTE When you restore files from the DAT drive, the software reads the directory, winds the tape to the spot where the requested files begin, and copies the files to the hard disk.

CHAPTER
16

How a Drive Array Works

DRIVE ARRAYS WORK on the theory that if one hard drive is a good thing, two hard drives are twice as good, and five hard drives are five times as good. By using multiple hard drives configured so the operating system thinks they are only a single drive, a personal computer can achieve greater speed reading data from the drives or greater protection from data loss. Ideally, you can achieve both economically.

The most common type of drive array is a *RAID*, an acronym for *redundant array of inexpensive drives*. The cost of hard drives increases with capacity and speed. But with a RAID, you can use several cheaper drives whose total cost is less than one high-performance drive and attain similar performance with greater data security.

RAIDs use some combination of mirroring and/or striping; both methods provide greater protection from lost data. *Mirroring*, in which one drive is a direct copy of another drive, provides the greatest performance enhancement but at the greatest cost. *Striping*, in which files are spread over several drives and protected with data on still another drive, is used when data protection is needed but performance is not a high priority.

Traditionally, drive arrays have been used only rarely on stand-alone PCs because, despite the tactic of using low-cost drivers, the array as a whole is still expensive compared to the cost of most individual PC components. Arrays are almost always found on PCs used as network servers.

Mirrored Drive Array

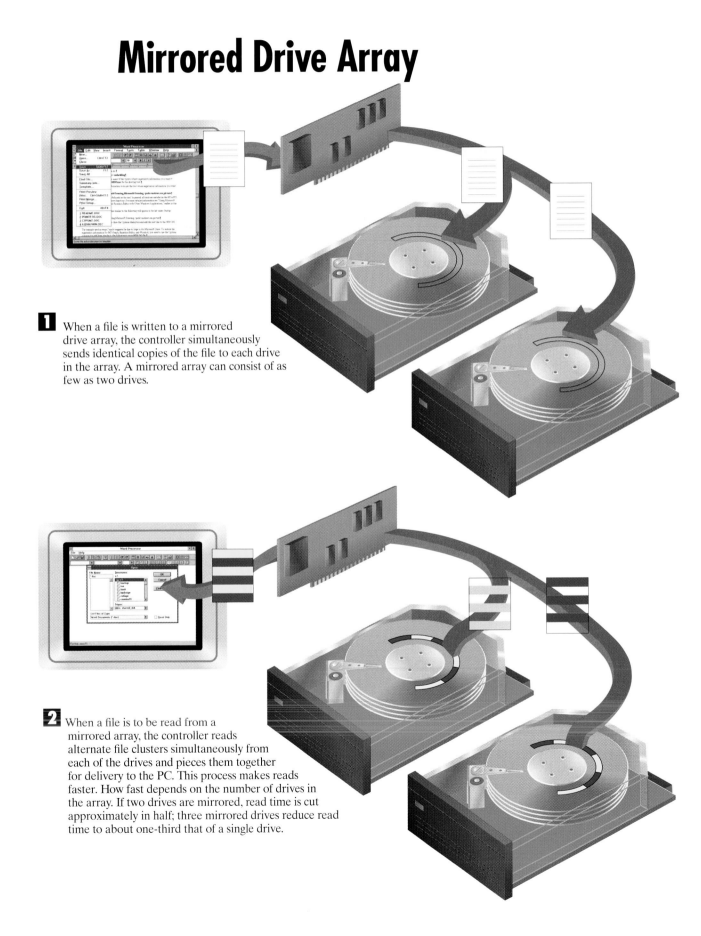

1 When a file is written to a mirrored drive array, the controller simultaneously sends identical copies of the file to each drive in the array. A mirrored array can consist of as few as two drives.

2 When a file is to be read from a mirrored array, the controller reads alternate file clusters simultaneously from each of the drives and pieces them together for delivery to the PC. This process makes reads faster. How fast depends on the number of drives in the array. If two drives are mirrored, read time is cut approximately in half; three mirrored drives reduce read time to about one-third that of a single drive.

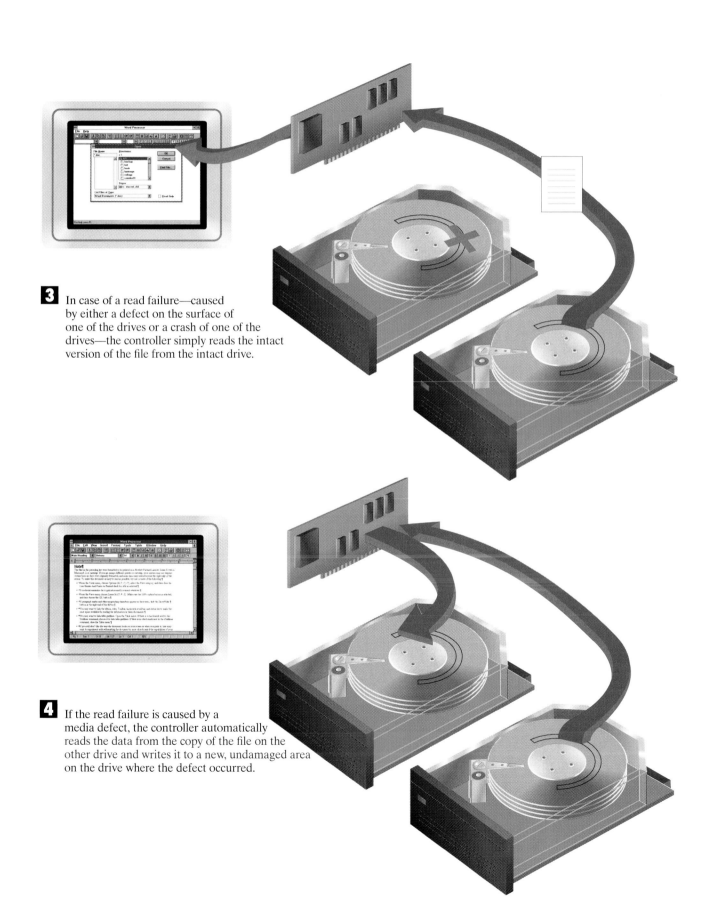

3 In case of a read failure—caused by either a defect on the surface of one of the drives or a crash of one of the drives—the controller simply reads the intact version of the file from the intact drive.

4 If the read failure is caused by a media defect, the controller automatically reads the data from the copy of the file on the other drive and writes it to a new, undamaged area on the drive where the defect occurred.

Striped Drive Array

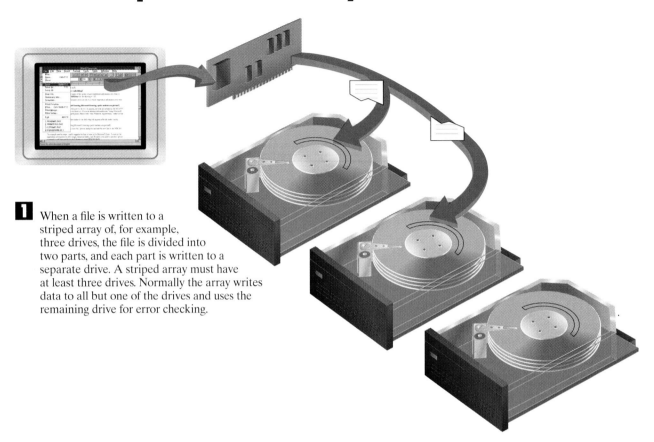

1 When a file is written to a striped array of, for example, three drives, the file is divided into two parts, and each part is written to a separate drive. A striped array must have at least three drives. Normally the array writes data to all but one of the drives and uses the remaining drive for error checking.

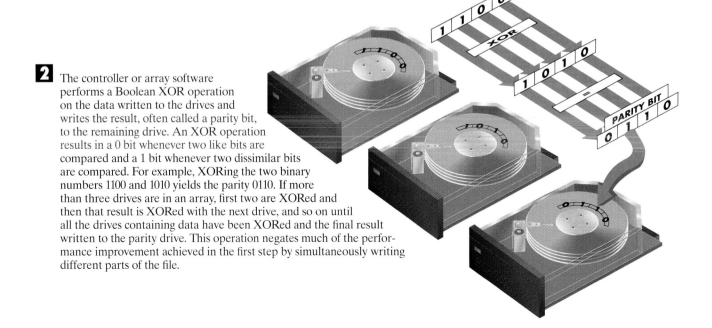

2 The controller or array software performs a Boolean XOR operation on the data written to the drives and writes the result, often called a parity bit, to the remaining drive. An XOR operation results in a 0 bit whenever two like bits are compared and a 1 bit whenever two dissimilar bits are compared. For example, XORing the two binary numbers 1100 and 1010 yields the parity 0110. If more than three drives are in an array, first two are XORed and then that result is XORed with the next drive, and so on until all the drives containing data have been XORed and the final result written to the parity drive. This operation negates much of the performance improvement achieved in the first step by simultaneously writing different parts of the file.

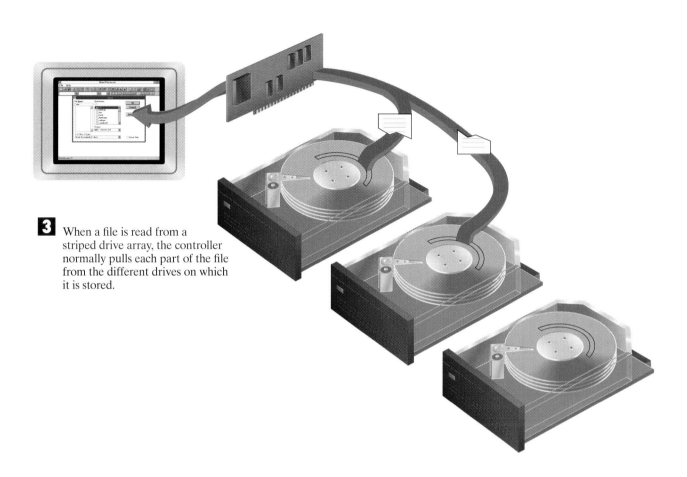

3 When a file is read from a striped drive array, the controller normally pulls each part of the file from the different drives on which it is stored.

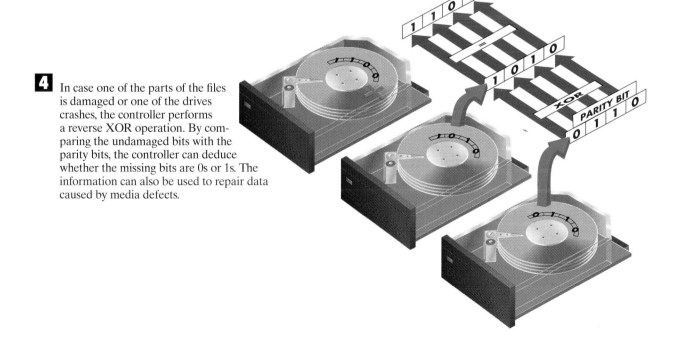

4 In case one of the parts of the files is damaged or one of the drives crashes, the controller performs a reverse XOR operation. By comparing the undamaged bits with the parity bits, the controller can deduce whether the missing bits are 0s or 1s. The information can also be used to repair data caused by media defects.

INPUT/OUTPUT DEVICES

CONTENTS

OVERVIEW

ALL THE MARVELOUS tasks that a personal computer is capable of doing would be meaningless without some way for the PC to communicate with the world outside of it. The first personal computers, such as the Altair, used a method of communicating so primitive that it's a wonder computing pioneers had the imagination to conceive that these contraptions could be practical in the real world. Program instructions and data were fed into the computer by flipping electrical switches—not miniaturized switches in the form of transistors but ordinary thumb-sized switches. The results of a computation were presented in the form of a seemingly random pattern of tiny light bulbs lit on a panel.

Today, the ways in which we communicate with a PC encompass devices that even the more imaginative of personal computing pioneers didn't envision. Keyboards and cathode-ray tubes (CRTs) are so common that we can't imagine a PC without them. In addition, there are modems, scanners, and mice, which help us obtain information and instructions from the outside world. In addition to the common CRT, there are a wide variety of state-of-the-art displays, including SuperVGA and active matrix color, and printers capable of far more than tapping out crude letters. So, today, you have a personal computer that is part of the real world, something you treat more like a person—someone who listens and replies to you—than you'd treat any other collection of microchips and electronics.

Strictly speaking, most devices outside the microprocessor itself—the largest part of a PC, in other words—are input or output devices. Each act of reading or writing data on a disk drive or in memory uses the services of the computer's BIOS (Basic Input/Output System). Still, we tend to associate input and output only with the devices, such as keyboard, monitor, and mouse, that we depend upon to do useful work. Our myopic view of what makes up input and output devices is understandable, for without those devices, even the most powerful PC imaginable would be nothing more than an awkward tool for the dedicated and a curiosity for the rest of us.

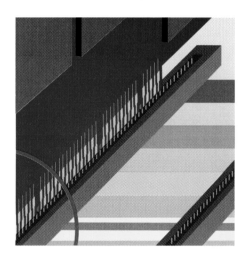

CHAPTER

How a Bus Works

ONE OF THE smartest ideas behind personal computers is *expansion slots*—plug-in connectors that allow you to insert additional circuit boards that attach to the rest of the PC through special circuitry called the *bus*. Expansion slots can transform personal computers so that they can do tasks never imagined by their designers. By inserting the right circuit board—usually called an *adapter* or an *expansion card*—you can increase the resolution and the number of colors used by the display, or you can transform your PC into a machine for recording and playing music, or you can make your PC operate drives, printers, tape backups, and a host of peripherals that didn't even exist when you bought the computer. The bus circuity is also used to communicate with some peripherals—such as the keyboard—that are not attached to an expansion board.

The advantages of an expansion bus are so obvious that you'd think all computers have them. But many computers before the introduction of the IBM PC had all their components hard-wired; that is, they could not be changed. Their designers, rather egotistically, decided they had produced the ultimate design and couldn't imagine that anyone would want to add something to it.

When IBM introduced its first PC, however, IBM was smart enough not only to make the computer expandable but also to make public most of the technical information that other companies would need to create expansion cards for the IBM PC. The result was an unprecedented flood of components that, to this day, continue to push the boundaries of what you can do with a personal computer.

The bus has become, along with the microprocessor in a PC, the most critical factor in performance and in differentiation among classes of computers. The directions taken by the development of buses will determine how well your future PCs work.

Differences in Buses

8-Bit Bus Data is transmitted to expansion slots and other components on the bus only along 8 parallel data lines.

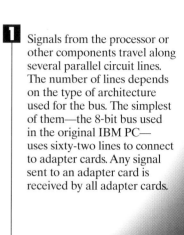

1 Signals from the processor or other components travel along several parallel circuit lines. The number of lines depends on the type of architecture used for the bus. The simplest of them—the 8-bit bus used in the original IBM PC— uses sixty-two lines to connect to adapter cards. Any signal sent to an adapter card is received by all adapter cards.

16-Bit or ISA Bus Data is transmitted along either 8 or 16 data lines, depending on what kind of adapter card is used in an expansion slot.

EISA or MCA Bus Data is transmitted along 32 data lines to adapter cards designed specifically to work with the 32-bit buses. MCA expansion slots cannot accept 8-bit or 16-bit adapter cards.

EISA Adaptability The design of EISA expansion slots allows 8-bit or 16-bit boards to enter only far enough to make contact with a row of 16 connectors that handle data based on the ISA bus. But boards designed specifically for the EISA slot can enter farther and align their connectors with 32 special slot connections that handle data based on EISA specifications.

8 If the signals on the address lines match the address used by an adapter, the adapter accepts the data sent on the address lines and uses that data to complete the write command.

7 The I/O adapters alerted by the write command turn their attention to the address lines. If the address specified on those lines is not the address used by an adapter, the adapter ignores the signals sent on the data lines.

Data Traveling along the Bus

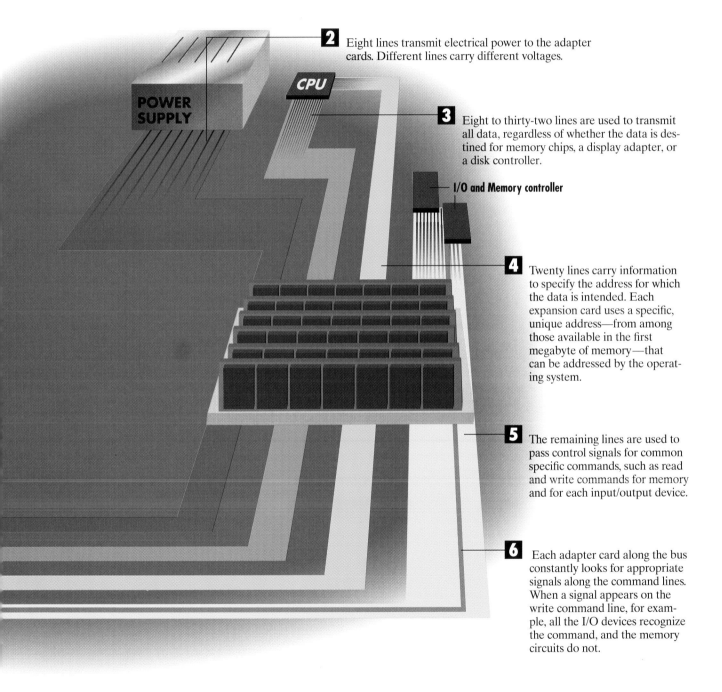

2 Eight lines transmit electrical power to the adapter cards. Different lines carry different voltages.

3 Eight to thirty-two lines are used to transmit all data, regardless of whether the data is destined for memory chips, a display adapter, or a disk controller.

I/O and Memory controller

4 Twenty lines carry information to specify the address for which the data is intended. Each expansion card uses a specific, unique address—from among those available in the first megabyte of memory—that can be addressed by the operating system.

5 The remaining lines are used to pass control signals for common specific commands, such as read and write commands for memory and for each input/output device.

6 Each adapter card along the bus constantly looks for appropriate signals along the command lines. When a signal appears on the write command line, for example, all the I/O devices recognize the command, and the memory circuits do not.

NOTE Recently a new way of communicating with peripherals has gained popularity. Called *local bus*, the design overcomes the speed limitation imposed on all other bus designs. The original bus was designed to run at 8MHz, which was roughly twice as fast as the original IBM PC's 8088 processor. As processor speeds increased to 10MHz, 25MHz, 33MHz, 50 MHz and faster, the bus speed stayed at 8MHz. The local bus is designed to transmit 32 bits of data at the local speed of a PC's processor. Usually a PC with a local bus limits that architecture to one or two slots, used for display adapters or disk controllers, where speed is most crucial. Slower conventional expansion slots are used to communicate with the serial and parallel ports and with the keyboard, where speed is not crucial.

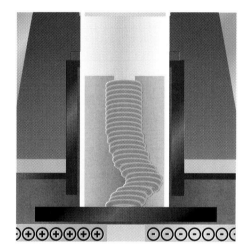

CHAPTER

18

How a Keyboard Works

YOU COME INTO direct contact with your PC's keyboard more than you do with any other component. You may go for years without ever seeing—much less touching—your PC's processor or hard drive, but most people pay much more attention to those components than they do to the one part of the computer that determines not how well the computer works but how well they work.

A poorly designed keyboard acts as a constant stumbling block to productivity and can even cause health problems. A well-designed keyboard is one that you never think about; your thoughts seem to flow directly from your mind to the computer's screen without you being aware of what your fingers are doing.

Despite the importance of the keyboard, most manufacturers—and too many users—pay little attention to it. Some keyboards these days are equipped with built-in trackballs or some other sort of pointing device, and some keyboards offer different slopes, which designers hope will help avoid repetitive-motion syndrome. The few radical changes that have appeared—concave keyboards with their keys equidistant from the fingers or keyboards that can be operated with one hand—have not caught on.

Regardless of whether it's because manufacturers are unimaginative or that computer users just don't care, the basic way a keyboard works has not changed significantly since the first IBM PC was introduced in the early 1980s. Although the layout of all keys except the alphanumeric ones is up for grabs—particularly on notebook keyboards—the only practical difference in how keyboards work is the mechanism that converts a key cap's movement into a signal sent to the computer. We'll look at both common key mechanisms: capacitive and hard contact. Except for this difference, the movement of the signal through the rest of the keyboard and your PC is a time-tested technology.

Capacitive Keys

1 In a *capacitive* keyboard, pressing the key cap compresses a spring and causes a plastic and metal plunger to move nearer to two pads that have large areas plated with a combination of tin, nickel, and copper. The pads are connected to the keyboard's printed circuit board. Although the two metallic areas never touch, they do act as a capacitor, with one pad maintaining a positive charge and the other, an equal negative charge. The collapse of the spring on some keyboards is designed so that it creates a mechanical click.

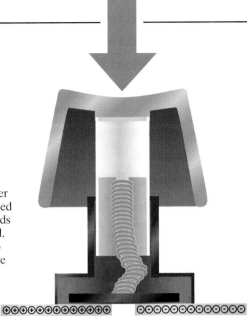

2 The metal plunger passing between the pads lowers the amount of the charge on the two pads. The difference in the charge causes a small, but detectable current to flow through the circuitry connected to the pads.

3 When the key cap is released, the spring expands, returning the key cap to its original height and moving the plunger away from the metallic pads, causing the current—flowing through the circuits leading to the pads—to return to its original level.

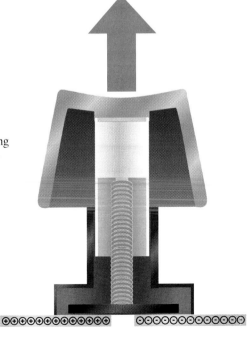

Hard-Contact Keys

1 In a *hard-contact* keyboard, pressing the key cap collapses a foam rubber dome.

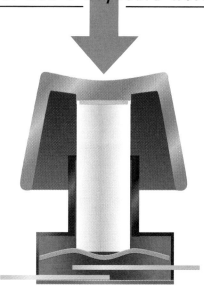

2 The collapsed dome presses against a sheet of plastic on the bottom of which is a metallic area connected to the rest of the keyboard's circuit board. The metallic surface contacts a similar surface on another plastic sheet, permitting current to flow through the printed circuits connected to each of the pads.

3 When the key cap is released, the rubber dome springs back to its original shape, releasing pressure on the plastic sheet. The plastic also returns to its original position, breaking the electrical circuit and cutting off the flow of current.

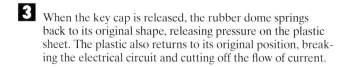

The Keyboard and Scan Codes

2 A microprocessor, such as the Intel 8048, built into the keyboard constantly scans circuits leading to the key caps. It detects the increase or decrease in current from the key that has been pressed. By detecting either an increase or a decrease in current, the processor can tell both when a key has been pressed and when it's been released. Each key has a unique set of codes, even if to the users, the keys seem identical. The processor can, for example, distinguish between the left and right shift keys. To distinguish between a real signal and an aberrant current fluctuation, the scan is repeated hundreds of times each second. Only signals detected for two or more scans are acted upon by the processor.

3 Depending on which key's circuit carries a signal to the microprocessor, the processor generates a number, called a *scan code*. There are two scan codes for each key, one for when the key is depressed and the other for when it's released. The processor stores the number in the keyboard's own memory buffer, and it loads the number in a port connection where it can be read by the computer's BIOS. Then the processor sends an interrupt signal over the keyboard cable to tell the processor that a scan code is waiting for it. An interrupt tells the processor to drop whatever else it is doing and to divert its attention to the service requested by the interrupt.

1 Regardless of which type of key cap is used, pressing it causes a change in the current flowing though the circuits associated with that key cap.

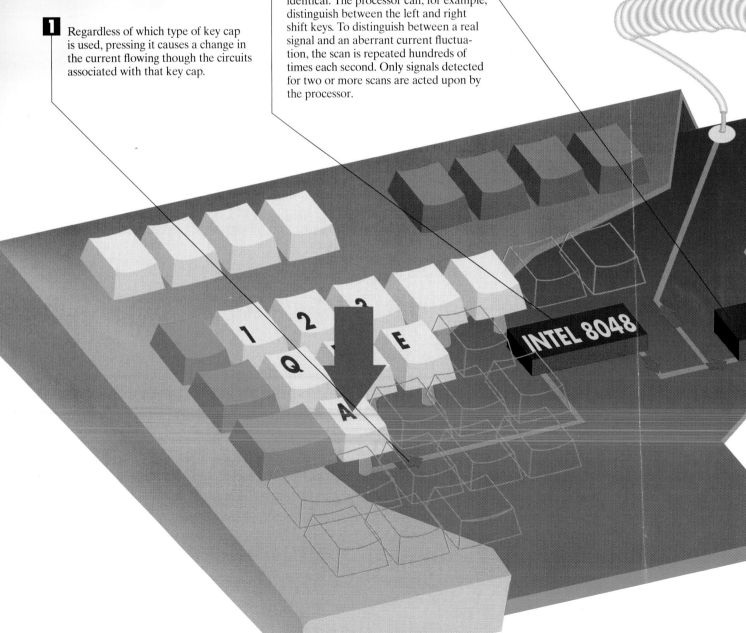

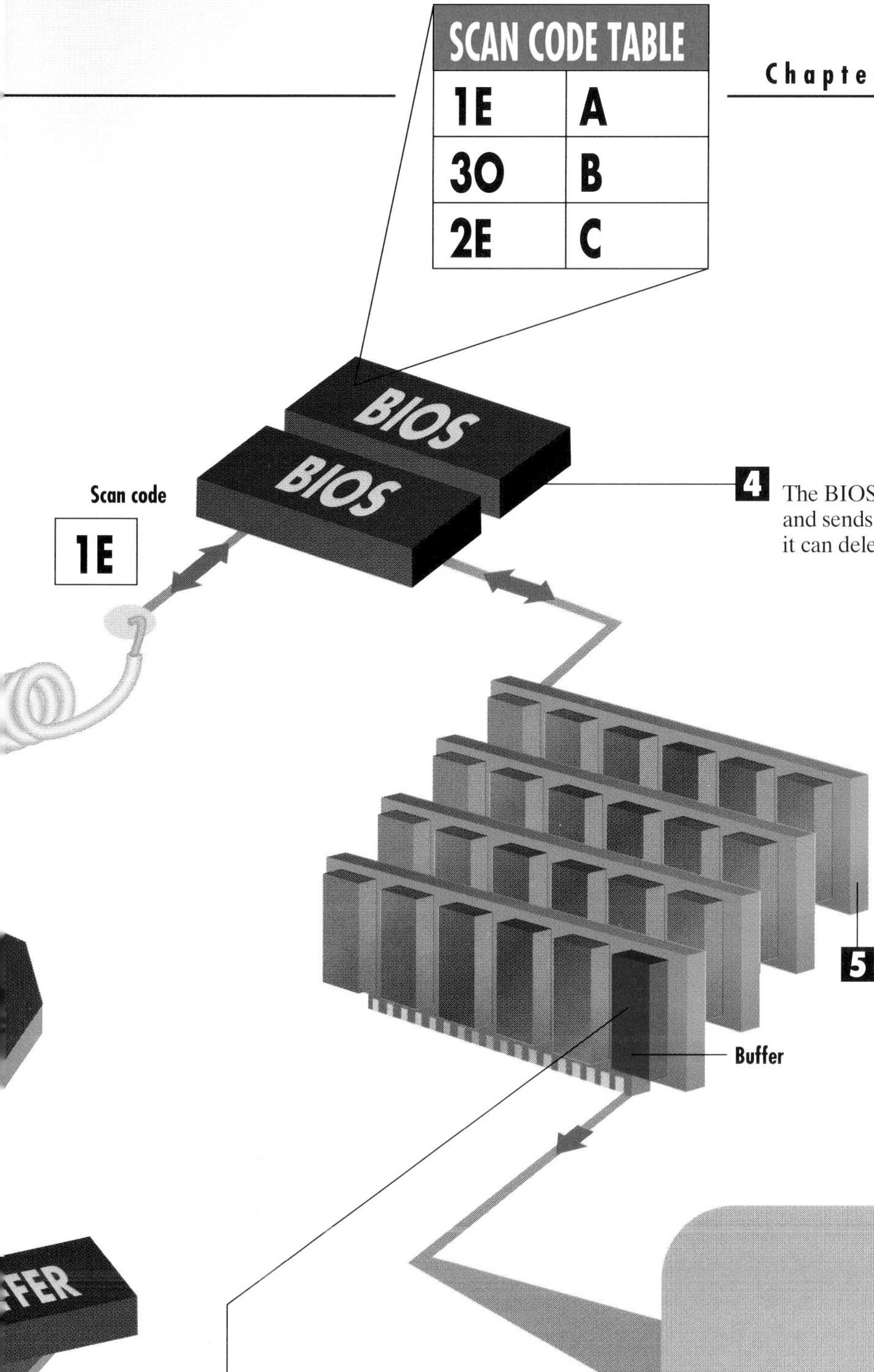

SCAN CODE TABLE

1E	A
30	B
2E	C

BIOS

BIOS

Scan code

1E

4 The BIOS reads the scan code from the keyboard port, and sends a signal to the keyboard that tells the keyboard it can delete the scan code from its buffer.

5 If the scan code is for one of the ordinary shift keys or for one of the keys that are considered to be special shift keys and toggle keys—Ctrl, Alt, Num Lock, Caps Lock, Scroll Lock, or Insert—the BIOS changes two bytes in a special area of memory to maintain a record of which of these keys has been pressed.

Buffer

6 For all other keys, the BIOS checks those bytes to determine the status of the shift and toggle keys. Depending on the status indicated by those bytes, the BIOS translates the appropriate scan code into an ASCII code, used by the PC, that stands for a character or into a special code for a function key or a cursor movement key. Uppercase and lowercase characters have different ASCII codes. In either case, the BIOS places the ASCII or special key code into its own memory buffer, where it is retrieved by the operating system or application software as soon as any current operation is finished.

A _

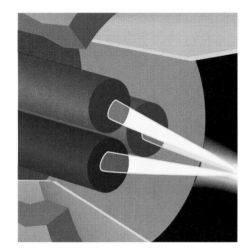

How a Computer Display Works

A FEW YEARS AGO, color monitors for personal computers were considered frivolous—more suited for playing games than doing real work. Most software was text based, and text produced by color displays was crude and difficult to read. Even for graphics applications, the color graphics adapter (CGA) monitors, which were the first color displays to appear for DOS-based computers, were seriously hindered by their inability to display more than 4 colors from a possible 16 in the monitor's highest resolution—a resolution filled with zigzags instead of smooth curves and straight lines.

Today, all that's changed. Not only is color considered acceptable for serious computing, but it's preferable in a computing arena that, with environments such as Windows and OS/2, is increasingly graphic. Software today uses color not simply to make itself prettier, but to convey more information.

Today's color displays are a far cry from the limited, crude color and graphics of only a decade ago. Instead of 4 colors, a palette of at least 256 colors is commonplace, and some displays provide thousands of colors. Instead of the CGA's Etch-a-Sketch–type resolution of 200 lines high by 640 pixels wide, modern displays provide resolutions of 768 lines high by 1,024 pixels wide, without breaking a sweat. (A *pixel*, short for *picture element*, is the smallest logical unit that can be used to build an image on the screen. A single pixel is usually created by several adjoining points of light. The fewer the dots of light used to create a pixel, the higher a monitor's resolution.)

The secret of today's better displays is a combination of the variable-graphics-array (VGA) display adapter and versatile monitors that can work with a variety of signals from the display adapter. Older display adapters used digital information exclusively, which meant that a display's pixel was either on or off, making it difficult to achieve subtle distinctions in colors. VGA uses an analog signal that converts digital information into different voltage levels that vary the brightness of a pixel. The process requires less memory and is more versatile. Super VGA displays use special chip sets and bigger memory to increase the number of colors and resolution even more.

Some form of VGA will be the standard for years to come. Here, we'll look at two types of VGA color displays—a desktop monitor and an LCD screen on a portable PC.

VGA Desktop Monitor

2 The DAC circuits compare the digital values sent by the PC to a look-up table that contains the matching voltage levels for the three primary colors needed to create the color of a single pixel. The table contains values for 262,144 possible colors, of which 256 values can be stored in the VGA adapter's memory. (Super VGA displays, which have more memory, can handle more colors and, for higher resolution, more pixels.)

3 The adapter sends signals to three electron guns located at the back of the monitor's cathode-ray tube (CRT). Each electron gun shoots out a stream of electrons, one stream for each of the three primary colors. The intensity of each stream is controlled by the signals from the adapter.

4 The adapter also sends signals to a mechanism in the neck of the CRT that focuses and aims the electron beams. Part of the mechanism, a *magnetic deflection yoke*, uses electromagnetic fields to bend the path of the electron streams. The signals sent to the yoke help determine the monitor's resolution—the number of pixels horizontally and vertically—and the monitor's *refresh rate*, which is how frequently the screen's image is redrawn.

VOLTAGES

RED	GREEN	BLUE	
5	2.5	1	
5	2.5	2	
5	2.5	3	
5	2.5	4	
5	2.5	5	

DAC

1 Digital signals from the operating environment or application software are received by the VGA adapter (sometimes built into the PC's motherboard). The adapter runs the signals through a circuit called a *digital-to-analog converter* (DAC). Usually the DAC circuit is contained within one specialized chip, which actually contains three DACs—one for each of the primary colors used in a display: red, blue, and green.

5 The beams pass through holes in a metal plate called a *shadow mask*. The purpose of the mask is to keep the electron beams precisely aligned with their targets on the inside of the CRT's screen. The CRT's *dot pitch* is the measurement of how close the holes are to each other; the closer the holes, the smaller the dot pitch. This, in turn, creates a sharper image. The holes in most shadow masks are arranged in triangles, with the important exception of those of the Sony Trinitron CRT used by many monitor manufacturers. The Trinitron's holes are arranged as parallel slots.

6 The electrons strike the phosphors coating the inside of the screen. (*Phosphors* are materials that glow when they are struck by electrons.) Three different phosphor materials are used—one each for red, blue, and green. The stronger the electron beam that hits a phosphor, the more light the phosphor emits. If each red, green, and blue dot in an arrangement is struck by equally intense electron beams, the result is a dot of white light. To create different colors, the intensity of each of the three beams is varied. After a beam leaves a phosphor dot, the phosphor continues to glow briefly, a condition called *persistence*. For an image to remain stable, the phosphors must be reactivated by repeated scans of the electron beams.

7 After the beams make one horizontal sweep across the screen, the electron streams are turned off as the electron guns refocus the paths of the beams back to the left edge of the screen at a point just below the previous scan line. The process is called *raster scanning*.

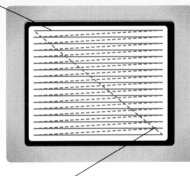

8 The *magnetic deflection yoke* continually changes the angles at which the electron beams are bent so that they sweep across the entire screen surface from the upper-left corner of the screen to the lower-right corner. A complete sweep of the screen is called a *field*. Upon completing a field, the beams return to the upper-left corner to begin a new field. The screen is normally redrawn, or refreshed, about 60 times a second.

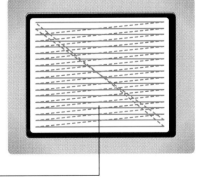

9 Some display adapters scan only every other line with each field, a process called *interlacing*. Interlacing allows the adapter to create higher resolutions—that is, to scan more lines—with less expensive components. But the fading of the phosphors between each pass can be more noticeable, causing the screen to flicker.

Color Liquid Crystal Display

2 A polarizing filter in front of the light panel lets through only the light waves that are vibrating more or less horizontally. The fact that the polarizing filter is not entirely precise allows the display to create different hues.

1 Light—emanating from a fluorescent panel behind a portable computer's display panel—spreads out in waves that vibrate in all directions.

3 In a layer of liquid-crystal cells, the built-in graphics adapter of the portable PC applies a varying electrical charge to some of the cells and no charge at all to other cells. In cells to which current is applied, the long, rod-shaped molecules that make up the liquid-crystal material react to the charge by forming a spiral. The greater the charge, the more that the molecules spiral. With the strongest charge, the molecules at one end of the cell wind up at an angle 90 degrees from the orientation of the molecules at the other end of the cell.

NOTE The model shown here is only one way in which liquid crystals and polarizers can manipulate light. Some LCD panels use two polarizers with the same alignment so that a charge applied to a liquid crystal cell results in light that's blocked because it's twisted. Also, two methods are used to apply charges to liquid crystal cells. *Passive matrix* displays use only a relatively few electrodes arranged as strips along the liquid crystal layer and rely on timing to make sure the correct cells are charged. The charges in passive matrix cells fade quickly, causing the colors to look faded. *Active matrix* displays, such as the one shown here, have individual transistors for each of the cells. The individual transistors provide a more precise and stronger charge, creating more-vivid colors. But active matrix is more expensive to produce because about 80 percent of the displays are currently rejected due to malfunctioning transistors.

4 Polarized light entering the cells from the rear is twisted along the spiral path of the molecules. In the cells to which a full charge was applied, the polarized light emerges vibrating at a 90-degree angle to its original alignment. Light passing through cells that have no charge emerges unchanged. Cells which received a partial charge twist the light to some angle between 0 and 90 degrees, depending on the amount of the charge.

5 The light emerging from each of the liquid-crystal cells passes through one of three color filters—red, blue, or green—that are arranged close to each other.

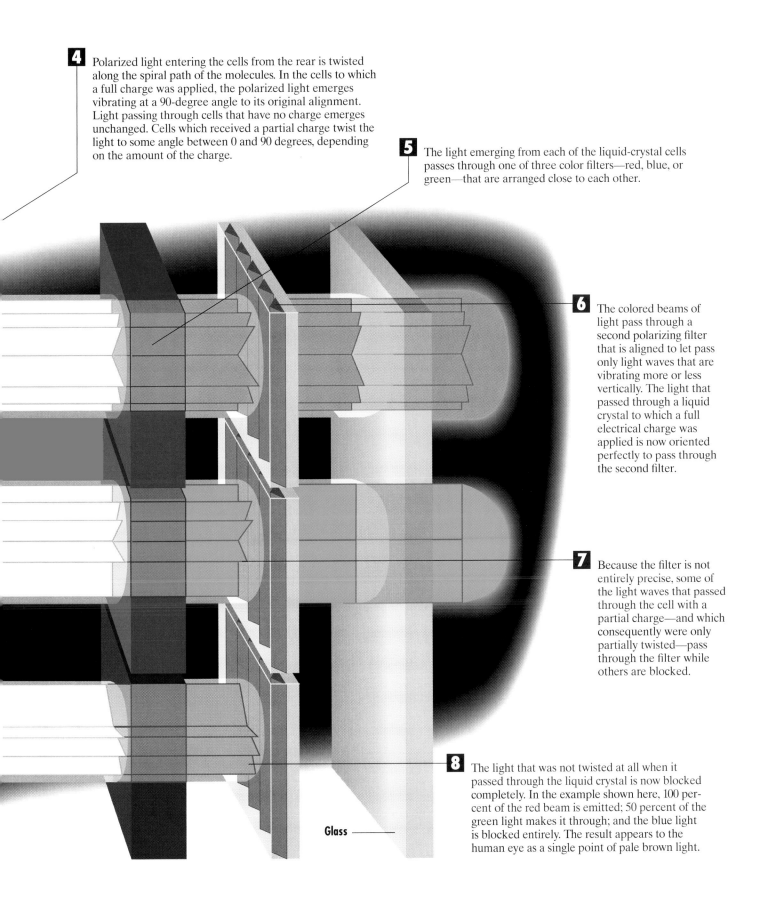

Glass

6 The colored beams of light pass through a second polarizing filter that is aligned to let pass only light waves that are vibrating more or less vertically. The light that passed through a liquid crystal to which a full electrical charge was applied is now oriented perfectly to pass through the second filter.

7 Because the filter is not entirely precise, some of the light waves that passed through the cell with a partial charge—and which consequently were only partially twisted—pass through the filter while others are blocked.

8 The light that was not twisted at all when it passed through the liquid crystal is now blocked completely. In the example shown here, 100 percent of the red beam is emitted; 50 percent of the green light makes it through; and the blue light is blocked entirely. The result appears to the human eye as a single point of pale brown light.

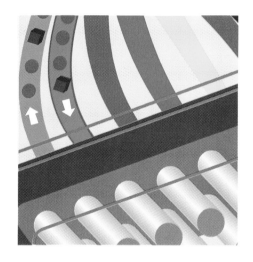

CHAPTER 20

How a Serial Port Works

WITHOUT A COMPUTER'S serial and parallel ports, much of the work that a PC accomplishes would never reach anyone other than the person sitting in front of the monitor. The serial port is the jack-of-all-trades among computer components. It is simple in concept: one line to send data, another line to receive data, and a few other lines to regulate how data is sent over the other two lines. Because of its simplicity, the serial port has been used at one time or another to make a PC communicate with just about any device imaginable—from commonplace modems and printers to plotters and burglar alarms.

The most common use for a serial port is with a mouse or modem. The reason for this is that a serial port is not a very efficient way to transfer data. It can only send data in series—one bit of data at a time, rather like soldiers marching single file. This inefficient data transfer, however, is acceptable for mice, which transmit so little data that speed is not crucial, and perfect for modems because, with current technology, phone lines cannot transport more than one signal at a time anyway.

The serial port is often referred to as an RS-232 port. RS-232 is the Electronics Industries Association's designation for a standard for how the various connectors in a serial port are to be used. The trouble is that the standard is often ignored by manufacturers of peripherals and even computer makers. The fact that both 9-pin and 25-pin connectors are used as serial ports shows we still have a long way to go before settling on exactly what constitutes an RS-232 port. The example shown here, which uses both types of connectors, depicts a serial port—connected to a modem—that conforms to the RS-232 standard.

Serial Port

3 Pin 4 on the PC connects to pin 20 on the modem. It signals that the PC is ready to receive data.

2 Pin 6—the same on both ends—sends a signal that data is ready to be sent.

1 Pin 1 and pin 5 on the computer's port connect, respectively, to pin 8 and pin 7 on the modem port. Pins 1 and 8 share a common ground connection. Pins 5 and 7 let the PC detect a phone-line signal.

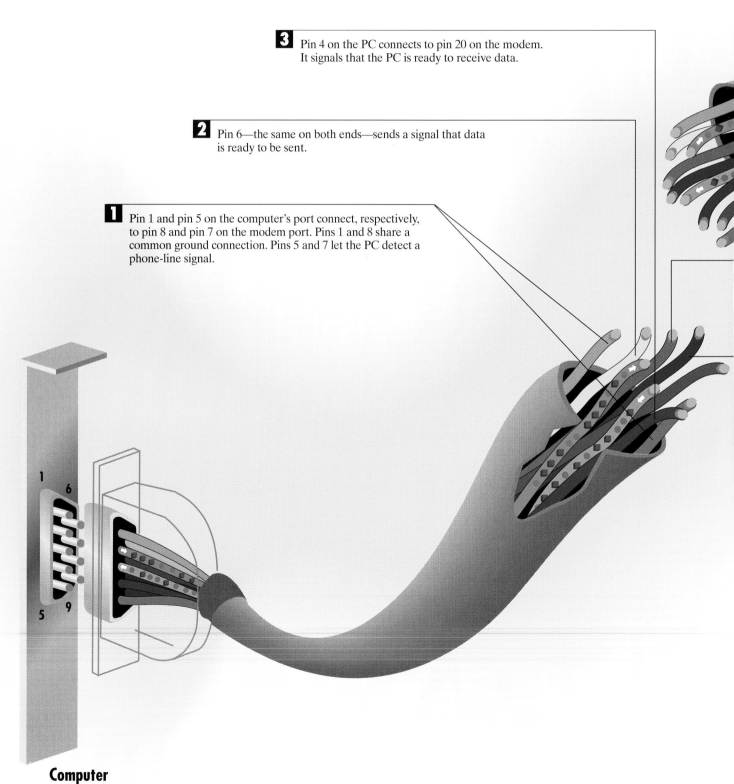

Computer

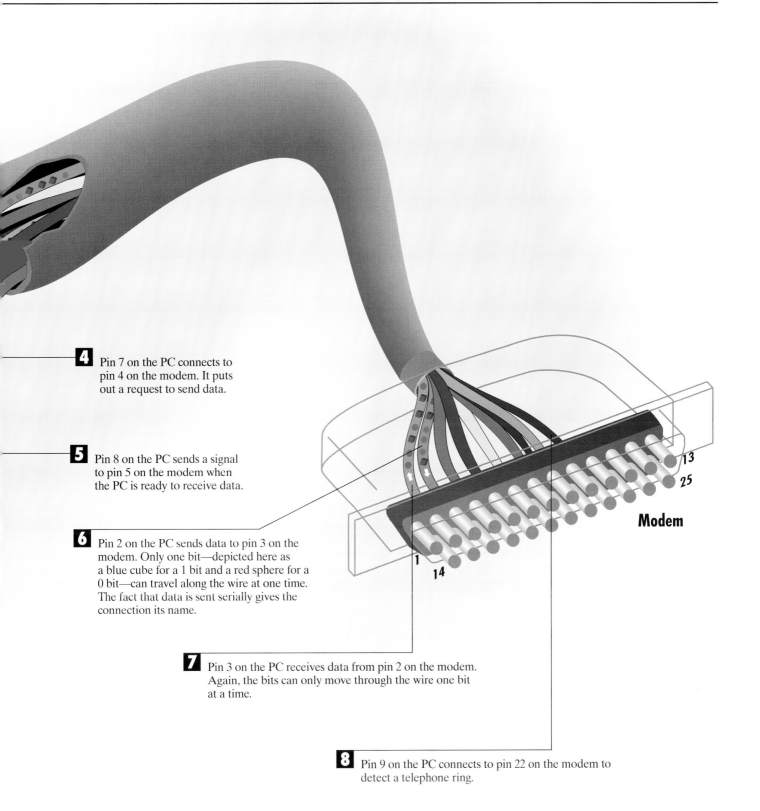

4 Pin 7 on the PC connects to pin 4 on the modem. It puts out a request to send data.

5 Pin 8 on the PC sends a signal to pin 5 on the modem when the PC is ready to receive data.

6 Pin 2 on the PC sends data to pin 3 on the modem. Only one bit—depicted here as a blue cube for a 1 bit and a red sphere for a 0 bit—can travel along the wire at one time. The fact that data is sent serially gives the connection its name.

Modem

7 Pin 3 on the PC receives data from pin 2 on the modem. Again, the bits can only move through the wire one bit at a time.

8 Pin 9 on the PC connects to pin 22 on the modem to detect a telephone ring.

How a Parallel Port Works

SINCE ITS INTRODUCTION, the *parallel port*—also often called a Centronics port—has been almost synonymous with *printer port*. Although a serial port can also be used to send data from a PC to some models of printers, the parallel port is faster. A serial port sends data one bit at a time over a single one-way wire; a parallel port can send several bits of data across eight parallel wires simultaneously, like soldiers marching several abreast. In the same time that a serial connection sends a single bit, a parallel port can send an entire byte. Or another way to look at it: In the time a serial connection can send the letter *A*, a parallel port can send the word *aardvark*.

A parallel connection has one drawback. The voltages in all its lines create *cross talk*, a condition in which the voltages leak from one line to another, just as you can sometimes hear someone else's phone conversation that has leaked into your own phone connection. Cross talk becomes worse the longer a parallel cable is; this limits most parallel connections to 10 feet.

Some early printers and plotters used serial ports to communicate with a printer. But today, graphics and scalable fonts are common in printed documents and they require that vast amounts of data be sent to the printer, making a parallel port the only practical choice. In addition, parallel ports are used for transporting files between two PCs, and the popularity of portable computers—which often lack any expansion slots—has created a market for peripherals such as drives and sound generators that can work off parallel ports.

Parallel Port

1 A signal to the PC on line 13—called the *select line*—from the peripheral, usually a printer, tells the computer that the printer is on line and ready to receive data.

2 Data is loaded on lines 2 through 9 in the form of a high voltage—actually about five volts—to signify a 1, shown here as a blue cube, and a zero or a low nearly zero voltage to signify a 0, shown as a red sphere.

3 After the voltages have been set on all the data lines, line 1 sends a strobe signal to the printer for one microsecond to let the printer know that it should read the voltages on the data lines.

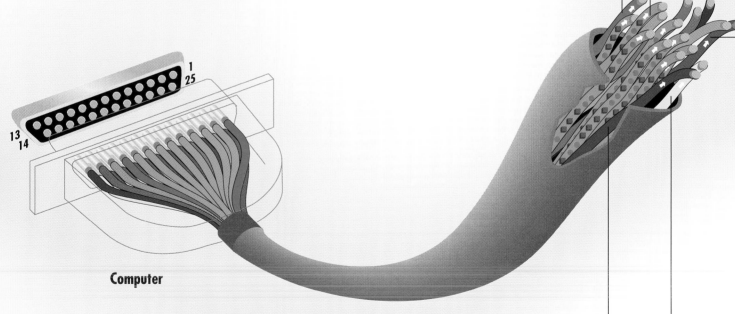

Computer

10 A signal from the PC on line 17 tells the printer not to accept data. This line is used only with some printers, which are designed to be switched on and off by the PC.

9 A low-voltage or zero-voltage signal from the PC on line 14 tells the printer to advance the paper one line when it receives a carriage return code. A high-voltage signal tells the printer to advance the paper one line only when it receives a line-advance code from the printer.

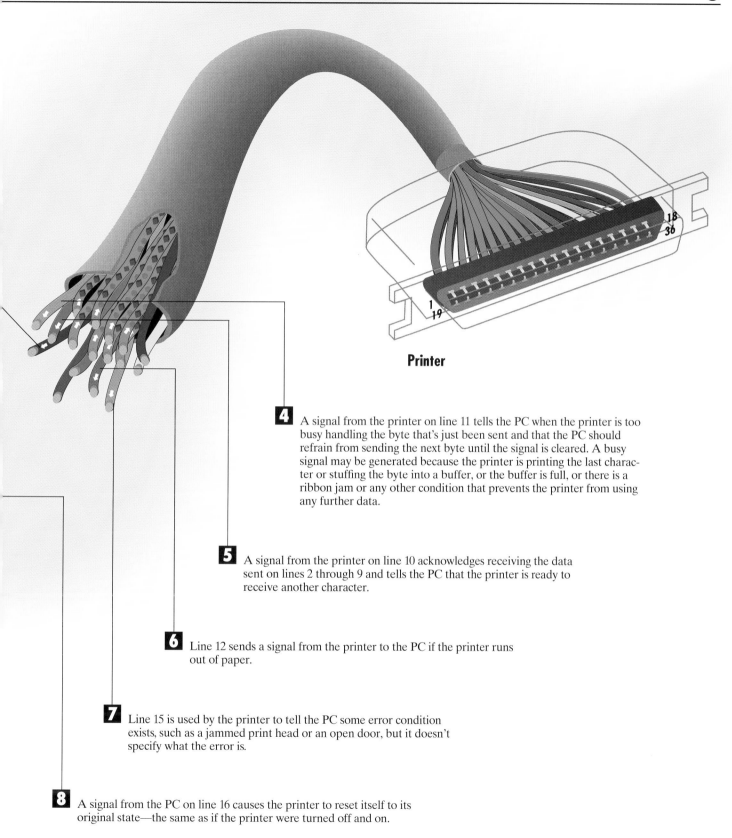

Printer

4 A signal from the printer on line 11 tells the PC when the printer is too busy handling the byte that's just been sent and that the PC should refrain from sending the next byte until the signal is cleared. A busy signal may be generated because the printer is printing the last character or stuffing the byte into a buffer, or the buffer is full, or there is a ribbon jam or any other condition that prevents the printer from using any further data.

5 A signal from the printer on line 10 acknowledges receiving the data sent on lines 2 through 9 and tells the PC that the printer is ready to receive another character.

6 Line 12 sends a signal from the printer to the PC if the printer runs out of paper.

7 Line 15 is used by the printer to tell the PC some error condition exists, such as a jammed print head or an open door, but it doesn't specify what the error is.

8 A signal from the PC on line 16 causes the printer to reset itself to its original state—the same as if the printer were turned off and on.

NOTE Lines 18 through 25 are simply ground lines.

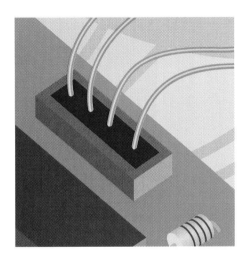

How a Mouse Works

THERE IS NOTHING natural or intuitive about a keyboard. No child is born knowing how to type, and even when the skill is learned, there's little sense to it—no one can give a good explanation of why the alphanumeric keys are arranged the way they are.

For many, the keyboard is a barrier to learning how to use a computer. Even for the experienced typist, there's nothing intuitive in typing /FS to save a file in Lotus 1-2-3. Engineers—not one of them touch typists, we'll bet—at Xerox Corporation's Palo Alto Research Center (PARC) developed a concept first explored by Douglas C. Engelbert of the Stanford Research Center. The concept was a *pointing device*, something a computer user could move with his or her hand, causing a corresponding move on screen. Because of its size and taillike cable, the device was named for the mouse. Apple Computer made the mouse a standard feature of its Macintosh computers, and with the popularity of Windows, a mouse is becoming standard equipment on all PCs, as well.

The mouse is not the only pointing device that's been invented. The joy stick used with games essentially accomplishes the same task, but doesn't feel quite right. Digitizing tablets are popular with architects and engineers who must translate precise movements of a pen into lines on the screen. Touch screens, on which you press either your finger or a special light pen to control the software, are too tiring to use for any length of time.

The mouse and its cousin, the trackball, have survived those other, more awkward methods of navigating with the keyboard. Mice can never replace the keyboard, but they can supplement the keyboard by doing tasks such as moving and pointing to on-screen objects, tasks for which the cursor keys are ill-suited. Until we reach the point where we simply talk to our PCs, mice will be an integral part of our systems.

The mechanical mouse has become the most popular pointing device for the newest breed of operating environments—graphic interfaces represented by Windows, the Macintosh, and OS/2. With the mouse, you control your PC by pointing to images instead of typing in commands. Here's how the mouse translates the movements of your hand into the actions on screen.

Mechanical Mouse

4 On the rims of each encoder are tiny metal contact points. Two pairs of contact bars extend from the housing of the mouse and touch the contact points on each of the encoders as they pass by. Each time a contact bar touches a point, an electrical signal results. The number of signals indicates how many points the contact bars have touched—the more signals, the farther you have moved the mouse. The direction in which the rollers are turning, combined with the ratio between the number of signals from the vertical and horizontal rollers, indicate the direction that the mouse is moving.

3 Each roller is attached to a wheel, known as an encoder, much like a car's drivetrain is attached by its axles to the wheels. As the rollers turn, they rotate the encoders.

2 As the ball rotates, it touches and turns two rollers mounted at a 90-degree angle to each other. One roller responds to back-and-forth movements of the mouse, which correspond to vertical movements on screen. The other roller senses sideways movements, which correspond to side-to-side movements on screen.

1 As you move a mechanical mouse by dragging it across a flat surface, a ball—made of rubber or rubber over steel—protruding from the underside of the mouse turns in the direction of the movement.

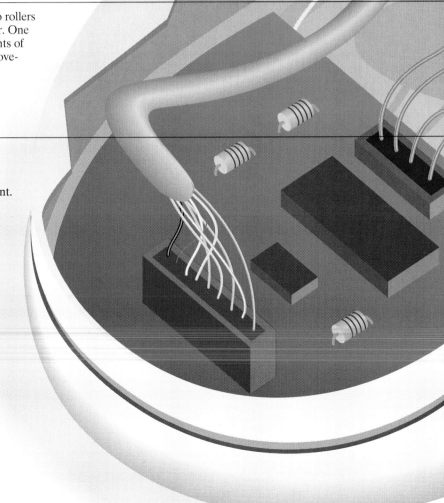

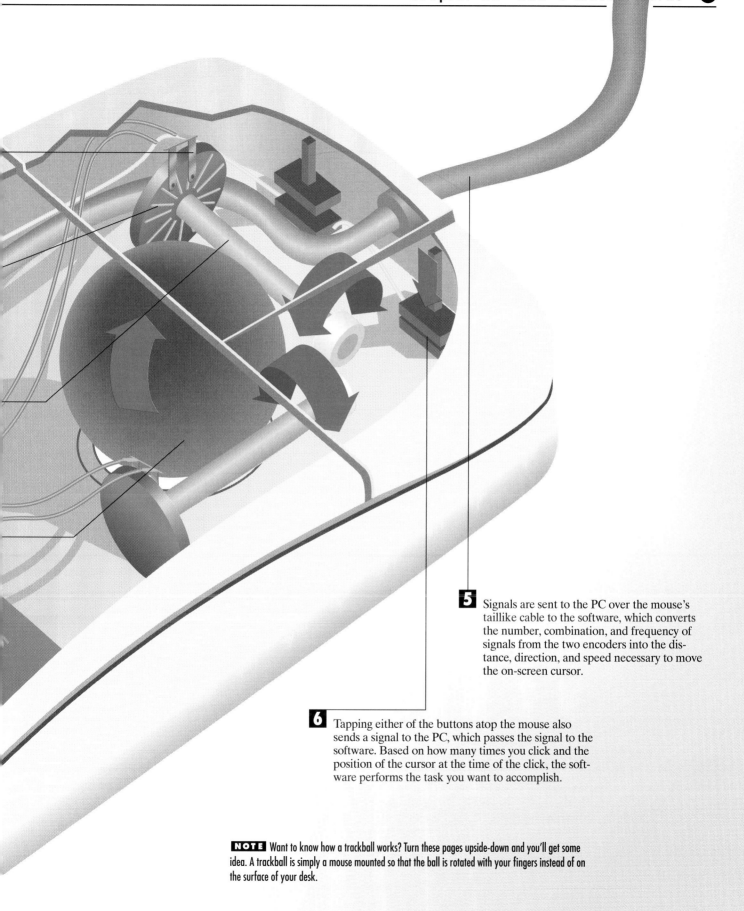

5 Signals are sent to the PC over the mouse's taillike cable to the software, which converts the number, combination, and frequency of signals from the two encoders into the distance, direction, and speed necessary to move the on-screen cursor.

6 Tapping either of the buttons atop the mouse also sends a signal to the PC, which passes the signal to the software. Based on how many times you click and the position of the cursor at the time of the click, the software performs the task you want to accomplish.

NOTE Want to know how a trackball works? Turn these pages upside-down and you'll get some idea. A trackball is simply a mouse mounted so that the ball is rotated with your fingers instead of on the surface of your desk.

How a Modem Works

YOUR PC IS a digital device. It accomplishes most of its tasks by turning on or off a series of electronic switches. A binary 0—shown here as a sphere—represents a switch that is turned off; a binary 1—a cube here—indicates that the switch is on. There is no in-between designation. A graph of digital code would look like this:

The telephone system is an analog device, designed—at a time when digital electronics was unknown—to transmit the diverse sounds and tones of the human voice. Those sounds are conveyed electronically in an analog signal as a continuous electronic current that smoothly varies its frequency and strength. It can be depicted on an oscilloscope as a wavy line, such as this:

A *modem* is the bridge between digital and analog signals. It converts on and off digital data into an analog signal by varying, or modulating, the frequency of an electronic wave, a process similar to that used by FM radio stations. On the receiving end of a phone connection, a modem does just the opposite: It demodulates the analog signals back into digital code. The two terms *MOdulate* and *DEModulate* give the modem its name.

Modem communications involve three of the least standardized elements of personal computing—serial ports, modem commands, and communications software (see "How a Serial Port Works"). The inconsistencies make it impossible to describe one universal way in which all modems work, but the operations discussed here accurately describe most software that uses a Hayes command-set modem with a 25-pin serial port.

Modem

1 Your communications software sends a voltage along pin 20 of the serial port to which the modem is connected. The voltage is called a *Data Terminal Ready* signal, or simply, a DTR signal. It tells the modem that the PC is turned on and ready to transmit data. At the same time, the PC detects a voltage from the modem on pin 6— *Data Set Ready*, or DSR signal—that lets the PC know the modem is ready to receive data or instructions. In a normal modem connection, both signals must be present before anything else can happen.

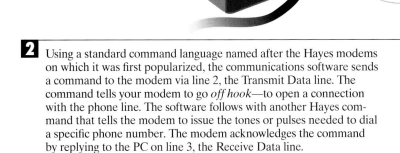

2 Using a standard command language named after the Hayes modems on which it was first popularized, the communications software sends a command to the modem via line 2, the Transmit Data line. The command tells your modem to go *off hook*—to open a connection with the phone line. The software follows with another Hayes command that tells the modem to issue the tones or pulses needed to dial a specific phone number. The modem acknowledges the command by replying to the PC on line 3, the Receive Data line.

3 When the modem on the other end of the phone connection—the remote modem—answers the call, your local modem sends out a hailing tone to let the remote modem know that it's being called by another modem. The remote modem responds with a higher-pitched tone. (You can ordinarily hear the two tones if your modem is equipped with a speaker.)

4 When communications are established, your modem sends your PC a *Carrier Detect* (CD) signal on line 8. The signal tells the communications software that the modem is receiving a *carrier signal*, which is a steady tone of a certain frequency and which later will be modulated to transmit data.

5 The two modems exchange information about how they'll send data to each other, a process called a *handshake*. The two modems must agree on the transfer speed, the number of bits that make up a *data packet*—for example, a single character—how many bits will signal the beginning and end of a packet, whether the modems will use a parity bit for error checking, and whether they will operate at *half-duplex* or *full duplex*. If the local and remote systems do not use the same settings, either they'll wind up sending characters that make no sense or they'll refuse to communicate at all. [*Continued on next page.*]

Frequency 1   Frequency 2   Frequency 3   Frequency 2

Transmission Speed Although transmission speeds are often expressed in *baud*—the number of frequency changes occurring during one second—that term is outdated and *bits per second* is more accurate today. The transmission rate on early modems of 300 bits per second was achieved by sending one frequency to indicate a 0 bit and a different frequency to indicate a 1 bit. The analog signal of a phone line is limited in how quickly it can switch frequencies, which has necessitated different schemes to increase the rate at which data is sent.

Group coding permits different frequencies to stand for more than one bit at a time. For 1,200 bit-per-second transmissions, for example, signals are actually sent at 600 baud, but four different frequencies are used to represent the four different possible pairs of binary bits: 0 and 0, 0 and 1, 1 and 0, and 1 and 1. A similar scheme matches more frequencies with more binary combinations to achieve 2,400 bits per second. For still faster transmission rates, the two modems must both use the same method of compressing data by recognizing frequently repeated patterns of 0s and 1s and using shorter codes to stand for those patterns.

Data Bits Communications systems may use either seven bits or eight bits to represent a data packet. In this example, eight data bits are used.

Data packet

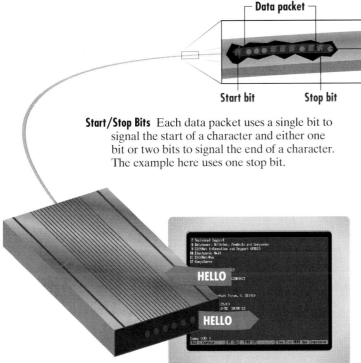

Start bit   Stop bit

Start/Stop Bits Each data packet uses a single bit to signal the start of a character and either one bit or two bits to signal the end of a character. The example here uses one stop bit.

Parity Bit As a form of error correction, the two systems may agree to use even parity, odd parity, or no parity at all. If they agree on even or odd parity, both systems add up the bits contained in the character and then add another bit called the parity bit. It may be either a 0 bit or a 1 bit, whichever is needed, to make the total either an even number or an odd number, depending on the parity that the systems agree on. The parity bits are used for error checking.

Half-/Full Duplex The two systems must agree which is responsible for displaying text on the local computer. One system must be set for full duplex and the other set for half-duplex. The system using full duplex is responsible for display text on both systems and echoes any text sent to it by the half-duplex system. If the two systems don't use complementary duplex settings, either no text will appear on the local system or each character will appear twice.

Modem

6 When the communications software wants to send data, it first sends voltage to line 4 on the serial port. This Request to Send (RTS) signal, in effect, asks if the modem is free to receive data from your PC. If the modem is receiving remote data it wants to pass on to your PC while your PC is busy doing something else, such as saving earlier data to disk, the PC will suspend the RTS signal to tell the modem to stop sending it data until the PC finishes its other work and reasserts the RTS signal

7 Unless your modem is too busy handling other data to receive new data from your system, it returns a Clear to Send (CTS) signal to your PC on serial port line 5, and your PC responds by sending the data to be transmitted on line 2. The modem sends data it received from the remote system to your PC via line 3. If the modem cannot transmit the data as fast as your PC sends data to it, the modem will drop the CTS signal to tell your PC to hold off on any further data until the modem catches up and renews the signal.

8 At the other end of the phone line, the remote modem hears incoming data as a series of tones with different frequencies. It demodulates these tones back into digital signals and sends them to the receiving computer. Actually, both computers can send signals back and forth at the same time because the use of a standard system of tones allows modems on either end to distinguish between incoming and outgoing signals.

9 When you tell your communications software to end a communications session, the software sends another Hayes command to the modem that causes it to break the phone connection. If the connection is broken by the remote system, your modem will drop the Carrier Detect signal to your PC to tell the software that communications are broken.

Reading Your Modem Lights

The indicator lights on the front of an external modem tell you what's happening during your communications session. The exact locations of the lights and the order in which they appear vary from modem to modem. But they are usually labeled with two-character abbreviations. Here's what they mean.

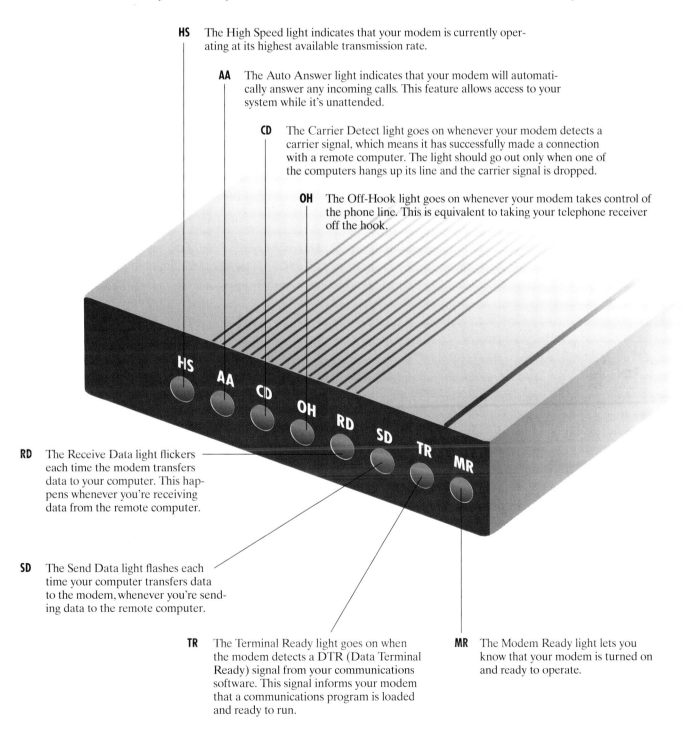

HS The High Speed light indicates that your modem is currently operating at its highest available transmission rate.

AA The Auto Answer light indicates that your modem will automatically answer any incoming calls. This feature allows access to your system while it's unattended.

CD The Carrier Detect light goes on whenever your modem detects a carrier signal, which means it has successfully made a connection with a remote computer. The light should go out only when one of the computers hangs up its line and the carrier signal is dropped.

OH The Off-Hook light goes on whenever your modem takes control of the phone line. This is equivalent to taking your telephone receiver off the hook.

RD The Receive Data light flickers each time the modem transfers data to your computer. This happens whenever you're receiving data from the remote computer.

SD The Send Data light flashes each time your computer transfers data to the modem, whenever you're sending data to the remote computer.

TR The Terminal Ready light goes on when the modem detects a DTR (Data Terminal Ready) signal from your communications software. This signal informs your modem that a communications program is loaded and ready to run.

MR The Modem Ready light lets you know that your modem is turned on and ready to operate.

How a Scanner and Optical Character Recognition Work

SCANNERS ARE THE eyes of your personal computer. They allow a PC to convert a drawing or photograph into code that a graphics or desktop publishing program can use to display the image on the screen, to reproduce the image with a graphics printer, or to convert pages of type into editable text.

The three basic types of scanners differ primarily in the way that the page containing the image and the scan head that reads the image move past each other. In a sheet-fed scanner, mechanical rollers move the paper past the scan head. In a flatbed scanner, the page is stationary behind a glass window while the head moves past the page, similar to the way a copying machine works. Hand-held scanners rely on the human hand to move the scan head.

Each method has its advantages and disadvantages. The flatbed scanner requires a series of mirrors to keep the image that is picked up by the moving scan head focused on the lens that feeds the image to a bank of sensors. Since no mirror is perfect, the image undergoes some degradation each time that it is reflected. But the advantage of a flatbed scanner is that it can scan oversized or thick documents, such as a book. However, with a sheet-fed scanner, the image is captured more accurately, but you're limited to scanning single ordinary-sized sheets.

A hand-held scanner is a compromise. It can scan pages in books, but often the scanning head is not as wide as that in either a flatbed or a sheet-fed scanner. Most hand-scanner software automatically combines two half-page scans into a single image. The hand-held scanner, dependent on the steadiness of your hand to accurately render an image, is generally less expensive because it doesn't require a mechanism to move the scan head or paper.

A scanner's sophistication lies in its ability to translate an unlimited range of analog voltage levels into digital values. Some scanners can distinguish between only black and white, useful just for text. More precise models can differentiate shades of gray. Color scanners use red, blue, and green filters to detect the colors in the reflected light.

Regardless of a scanner's sensitivity to gray or how the head and paper move, the operations of all scanners are basically simple and similar. We'll look at two that are representative of the technologies involved—a flatbed scanner and a hand-held grayscale scanner. We'll also examine one of the most important reasons for scanning a document—to convert its image into editable text by using optical character-recognition software.

Flatbed Scanner

1 A light source illuminates a piece of paper placed face down against a glass window above the scanning mechanism. Blank or white spaces reflect more light than do inked or colored letters or images.

6 The digital information is sent to software in the PC, where the data is stored in a format with which a graphics program or an optical character-recognition program can work.

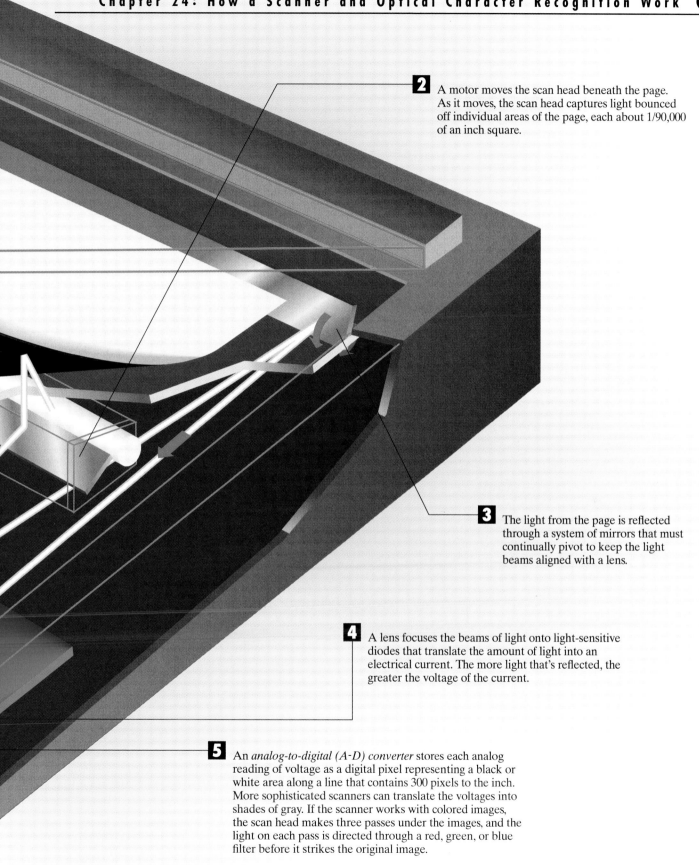

2 A motor moves the scan head beneath the page. As it moves, the scan head captures light bounced off individual areas of the page, each about 1/90,000 of an inch square.

3 The light from the page is reflected through a system of mirrors that must continually pivot to keep the light beams aligned with a lens.

4 A lens focuses the beams of light onto light-sensitive diodes that translate the amount of light into an electrical current. The more light that's reflected, the greater the voltage of the current.

5 An *analog-to-digital (A-D) converter* stores each analog reading of voltage as a digital pixel representing a black or white area along a line that contains 300 pixels to the inch. More sophisticated scanners can translate the voltages into shades of gray. If the scanner works with colored images, the scan head makes three passes under the images, and the light on each pass is directed through a red, green, or blue filter before it strikes the original image.

Hand-held Scanner

2 The lens focuses a single line of the image onto a *charge coupled device* (CCD), which is a component designed to detect subtle changes of voltage. The CCD contains a row of light detectors. As the light shines onto these detectors, each registers the amount of light as a voltage level that corresponds to white, black, gray, or to a color.

1 When you press the scan button on a typical hand-held scanner, a light-emitting diode (LED) illuminates the image beneath the scanner. An inverted, angled mirror directly above the scanner's window reflects the image onto a lens in the back of the scanner.

6 As the disk turns, a light shines through the slits and is detected by a photomicrosensor on the other side of the disk. Light striking the sensor throws a switch that sends a signal to the A-D converter. The signal tells the converter to send the line of bits generated by the converter to your PC. The converter clears itself of the data, and it is ready to receive a new stream of voltages from the next line of the image.

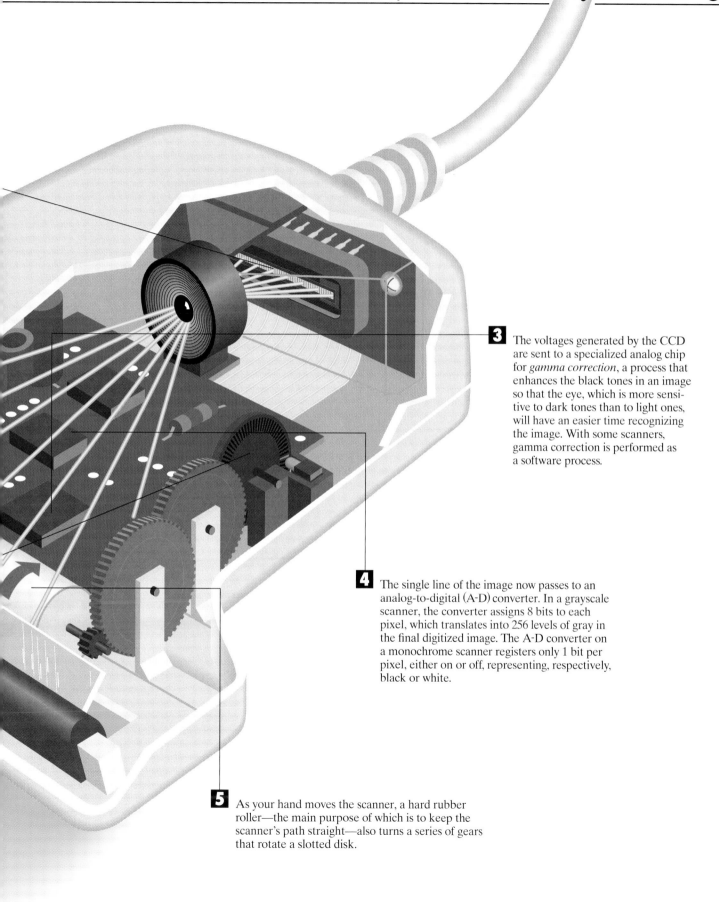

3 The voltages generated by the CCD are sent to a specialized analog chip for *gamma correction*, a process that enhances the black tones in an image so that the eye, which is more sensitive to dark tones than to light ones, will have an easier time recognizing the image. With some scanners, gamma correction is performed as a software process.

4 The single line of the image now passes to an analog-to-digital (A-D) converter. In a grayscale scanner, the converter assigns 8 bits to each pixel, which translates into 256 levels of gray in the final digitized image. The A-D converter on a monochrome scanner registers only 1 bit per pixel, either on or off, representing, respectively, black or white.

5 As your hand moves the scanner, a hard rubber roller—the main purpose of which is to keep the scanner's path straight—also turns a series of gears that rotate a slotted disk.

Optical Character Recognition

1 When a scanner reads-in the image of a document, the scanner converts the dark elements—text and graphics—on the page to a *bitmap*, which is a matrix of square pixels that are either on (black) or off (white). Because the pixels are larger than the details of most text, this process degenerates the sharp edges of characters, much as a fax machine blurs the sharpness of characters. This degradation creates most of the problems for optical character-recognition (OCR) systems.

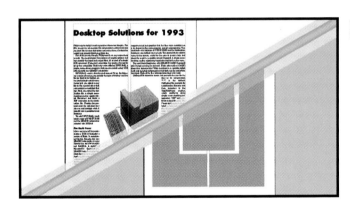

2 The OCR software reads-in the bitmap created by the scanner and averages out the zones of on and off pixels on the page, in effect, mapping the white space on the page. This enables the software to block off paragraphs, columns, headlines, and random graphics. The white space between lines of text within a block defines each line's baseline, an essential detail for recognizing the characters in the text.

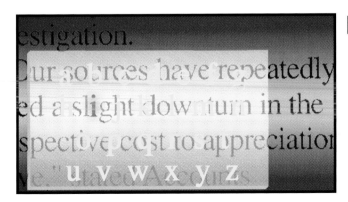

3 In its first pass at converting images to text, the software tries to match each character through a pixel-by-pixel comparison to character templates that the program holds in memory. Templates include complete fonts—numbers, punctuation, and extended characters—of such common faces as 12-point Courier and the IBM Selectric typewriter set. Since this technique demands a very close match, the character attributes, such as bold and italic, must be identical to qualify as a match. Poor-quality scans can easily trip up matrix matching.

4 The characters that remain unrecognized go through a more intensive and time-consuming process called *feature extraction*. The software calculates the text's *x-height*—the height of a font's lowercase *x*—and analyzes each character's combination of straight lines, curves, and bowls (hollow areas within loops, as in *o* or *b*). The OCR programs know, for example, that a character with a curved descender below the baseline and a bowl above it is most likely a lowercase *g*. As the software builds a working alphabet of each new character it encounters, recognition speed accelerates.

5 Because these two processes don't decipher every character, OCR programs take two approaches to the remaining hieroglyphics. Some OCR programs tag unrecognized characters with a distinctive character—such as ~, #, or @—and quit. You must use the search capability of a word processor to find where the distinctive character has been inserted and correct the word manually. Some OCR programs may also display a magnified bitmap on screen and ask you to press the key of the character needed to substitute for the placeholder character.

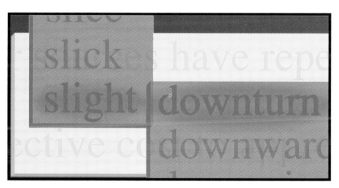

6 Still other OCR programs invoke a specialized spelling checker to search for obvious errors and locate possible alternatives for words that contain tagged unrecognized characters. For example, to OCR programs, the number *1* and the letter *l* look very similar, so do *5* and *S*, or *cl* and *d*. A word such as *downturn* may be rendered as *clownturn*. A spelling checker recognizes some typical OCR errors and corrects them.

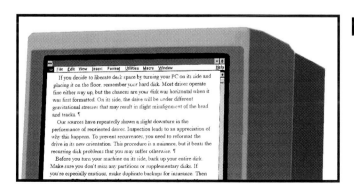

7 Most OCR programs give you the option of saving the converted document to an ASCII file or in a file format recognized by popular word processors or spreadsheets.

How a Pen-Based Computer Works

EVEN A MOUSE goes only so far toward eliminating the keyboard, which is the primary barrier to computer use for many people in many situations. That barrier is now being attacked by hand-held pen-based PCs.

The objective of pen-based computing is to emulate the common paper tablet and pen. About the width and length of a paper tablet, but usually thicker, a pen-based computer is held with one hand while the other hand uses a specialized stylus to write, draw, and make selections on a flat LCD screen. Anyone who can use a ballpoint pen should be able to use a pen-based computer.

To achieve this simplicity, a pen-based computer must accomplish two feats: It must recognize the movements of the pen and translate those movements into characters or meaningful functions. Pen-based operating systems recognize certain specific pen gestures that stand for specific actions, such as drawing a circle or deleting a word. They can also recognize characters that are written with painstaking precision, and they can be trained to recognize characters written in your own quirky penmanship.

Pen-based computing is still in an infant stage, and the processors used in many of them are not powerful enough to convert handwriting easily and quickly into ordinary text. For that reason, the applications that are most likely to be the first to appear on pen-based computers are those that lend themselves neatly to fill-in forms that can be completed largely by checking boxes and making menu choices; for example, traffic tickets and order forms.

But even when processing and software performance improve to the point that the actuality of pen-based computing is as good as its promise, the technology will remain largely the same as what we'll examine here. We'll look at two methods of detecting pen movements and a common way in which pen-based PCs incorporate those movements into text or actions.

Pen-Based Computer

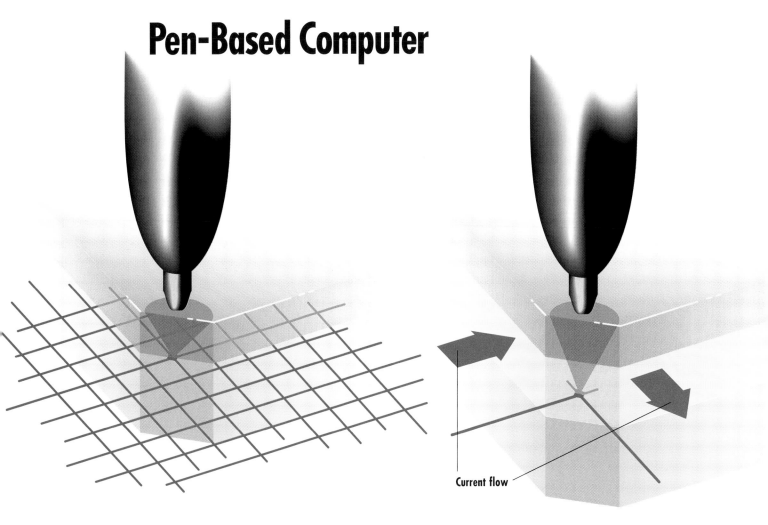

Current flow

Wire Grid Screens One type of pen computer uses an LCD screen in which a grid of wires is embedded. The voltage level of the current flowing through the wires changes when an electromagnetic field created by the pen passes over the wire.

Metallic Coated Screens Another type of pen-based computer uses an LCD screen coated with a transparent, metallic film. Electrical current flows through the film from the top of the screen to one of its sides. When the pen touches the screen, the pen's electromagnetic field creates a disturbance in the flow of current.

Both Types of Screens When the pen touches either type of screen, an electrical current in the pen generates its own electromagnetic field that changes the voltage of the current running through the wires or the metallic coating. The farther the pen is from the sides of the screen generating the current, the greater the voltage change. From the amount of change, the computer's processor identifies the X and Y coordinates of the pen on the screen and the direction of any movement [*see opposite page*].

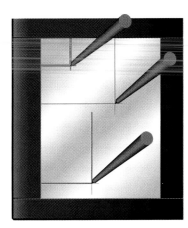

Character and Gesture Recognition

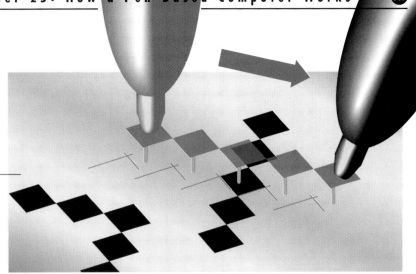

1 After reading the position of its pen, the computer sends a signal to the screen to turn on (or off, depending on the background color) the pixels at the pen's position, a process called *showing ink*. As the pen moves, the computer continually calculates its position and instructs other pixels to turn on. The computer distinguishes between pixels that match the pen's positions (called the *input plane*) and pixels that are turned on by the application (the *output plane*). Note that the screen does not contain two separate, physical levels of LCD pixels; rather, the distinction between input and output planes is a logical one. The same pixels are used for input and output planes, but the operating system tracks for which of the two logical planes the pixels are being used.

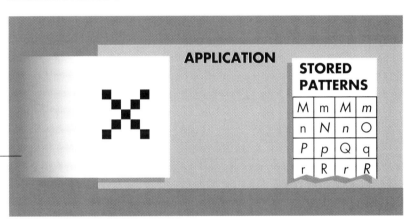

2 At the end of a pen stroke, the computer's operating system passes a description of the stroke to the application, which compares the pattern traced by the pen with a collection of other patterns that it recognizes. The software makes allowances for inexact matches so that the pattern drawn with the pen can be imprecise, within certain limits.

3 When the application encounters a pen pattern that resembles one of its stored patterns, the software considers the context in which the pen stroke was entered. For example, an *X* pattern entered in a blank space in the context of written words is interpreted as the letter *X*. If, however, the *X* pattern is placed over an existing word, the application interprets the pattern to mean that the word should be deleted. In the context of a check box, the application translates the *X* pattern to mean "fill in the check box."

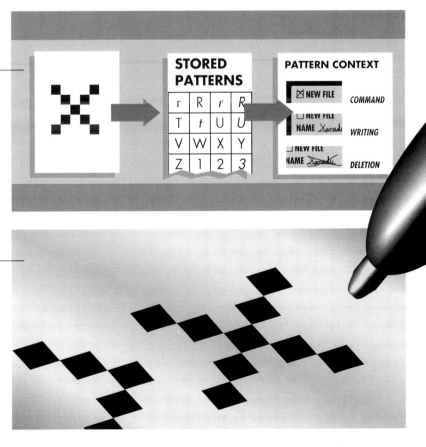

4 The application erases the pixel image on the input plane and replaces it by displaying on the output plane the pixel patterns that correspond to the software's interpretation of the patterns.

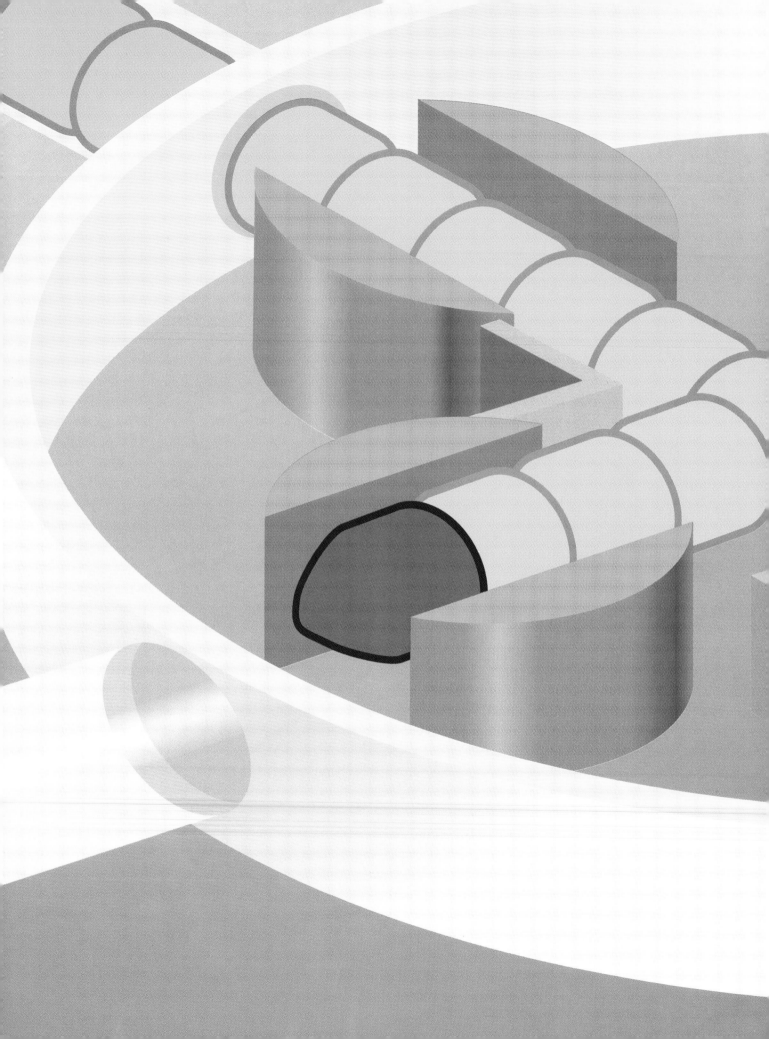

5

NETWORKS

C O N T E N T S

BEFORE THE EMERGENCE of the PC, there was the terminal—a rather dumb display—and a keyboard; these gave computer users at the same location access to the same centralized computer. Usually, that computer was a large, mysterious box off in some other room, where it was tended by specialists in white lab coats.

The system was not unlike some primitive religions in which the high priests were the only ones with the secret knowledge of how to communicate with their god. Mere users were forbidden to enter the temple and certainly could not address the computer god directly. The people sitting in front of the terminal had to be content with whatever blessings or curses the computer and its priests cared to bestow on them.

With the centralized computer, users had access to only the software that the MIS (management information system) personnel chose to install. Often getting a new type of information out of that software required submitting a written request to the MIS priests and then waiting weeks for the results.

The personal computer—at least initially—seemed to be the beginning of the centralized computer's downfall. PC users could install on a PC whatever software they liked. The information users could extract from a PC was limited mostly by their skill with the software. And many users found that computing was really like the "great and powerful" Wizard of Oz: Once they got a peek behind the curtain that MIS had placed around computing, they found computers were just machines that weren't intimidating, after all.

More and more of the work that used to be done on mainframes and minicomputers wound up on PCs. Generally that has been all to the good, but the move away from centralized computing has a downside. When individuals work on stand-alone PCs, they work with stand-alone information. They lose the benefits of access to the information on the PC in the office next door. If a coworker does something that affects the data on which a business is based, the stand-alone PC user is left alone in the dark. Individual PCs do not reflect one very important aspect of the way most of us work—in cooperation with others.

The need to communicate and to share information with others gave rise to the PC network. With a network, you can retain the benefits of a personal computer—your own selections of software and a place for personal data not for sharing—and regain the benefits of centralized computing. With a network, you and your coworkers have the ability to work with the same latest version of the company's data and share selected information and messages.

Combining the benefits of PCs with those of networks is not a simple matter. A network has to give most users access to most of the same information, but at the same time, it has to protect that data from the mistakes or misuse of any individual. The network becomes not only a link among personal computers—and often mainframes and minicomputers—but it must also act as a referee to arbitrate among conflicting requests for data and access to the network's resources.

Networking is new and arcane; it is filled with mysteries for most of those who use it. To explain all its workings, blessings, and failures would require its own book. Here we'll just examine some of the basics of network computing—how a network physically links individual PCs and referees their requests for attention and how a network creates a system of security to protect itself and its common data.

CHAPTER
26

How LAN Topologies Work

THE FUNDAMENTAL JOB of a LAN (local area network) is to physically link several PCs to each other and often to a mainframe or minicomputer. This is accomplished with a variety of materials—twisted-wire cables, fiber optics, phone lines, and even infrared light and radio signals.

There are nearly as many ways to link PCs logically as physically. Each network configuration—or *topology*—must still perform the same chores. The most common situation that a network encounters is a message from one PC to another. The message may be a query for data, the reply to another PC's data request, or an instruction to run a program that's stored on the network. (The process is actually more detailed than that. See the next chapter, "How Network Communications Work.")

The data or program that the message asks for may be stored on a PC used by a coworker on the network, or on a file server, a specialized PC. A *file server* is usually a high-performance PC with a large hard drive that is not used exclusively by any individual on the network. Instead, it exists only to serve all the other PCs using the network by providing a common place to store data that can be retrieved as rapidly as possible. Similarly, a network may include print servers that everyone on the LAN can use for printing. A *print server* is a PC connected to a printer or an intelligent printer that can be connected to a network without an intervening PC.

The network must receive requests for access to it from individual PCs, or *nodes*, linked to the network, and the network must have a way of handling simultaneous requests for its services. Once a PC has the services of the network, the network needs a way of sending a message from one PC to another so that it goes only to the node it's intended for and doesn't pop up on some other unsuspecting node. And the network must do all of this as quickly as possible while spreading its services as evenly as possible among all the nodes on the LAN.

Three network topologies—bus, token ring, and star—account for most LAN configurations. Here's how the three handle service requests and conflicts.

Bus Network

1 All nodes on a bus network are attached to the LAN as branches off a common line. Each node has a unique address. The network card installed in a node, which can be another PC, a file server, or printer server, listens to make sure that no other signals are being transmitted along the network. It then sends a message to another device by giving it to a *transceiver*. Each node has its own transceiver.

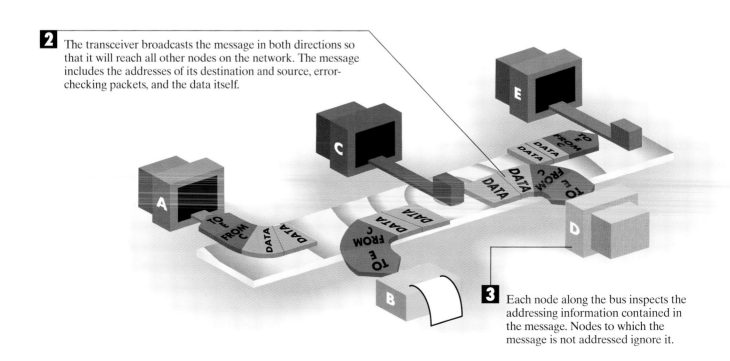

Transceiver

Nodes

2 The transceiver broadcasts the message in both directions so that it will reach all other nodes on the network. The message includes the addresses of its destination and source, error-checking packets, and the data itself.

3 Each node along the bus inspects the addressing information contained in the message. Nodes to which the message is not addressed ignore it.

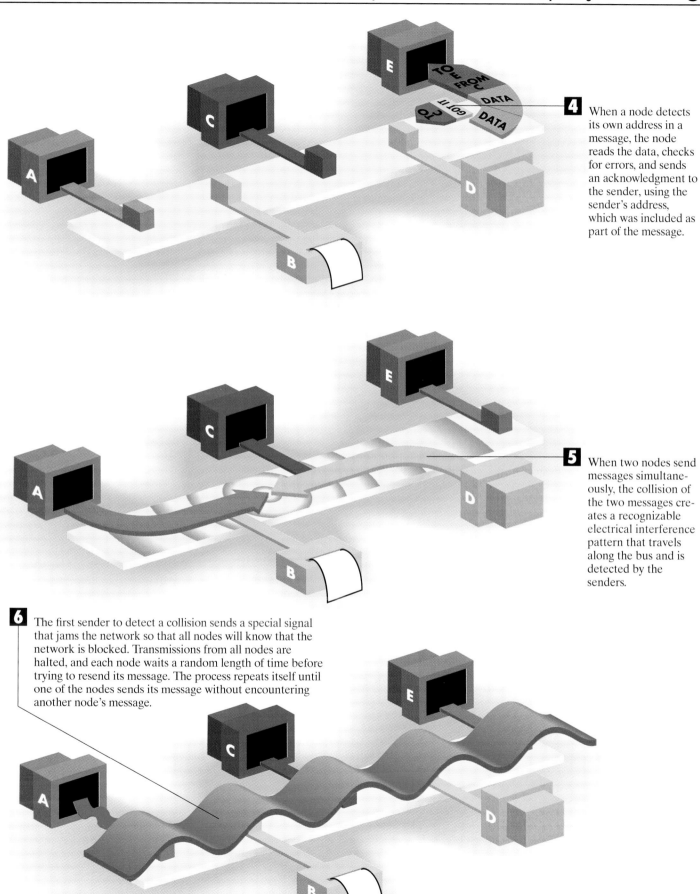

4 When a node detects its own address in a message, the node reads the data, checks for errors, and sends an acknowledgment to the sender, using the sender's address, which was included as part of the message.

5 When two nodes send messages simultaneously, the collision of the two messages creates a recognizable electrical interference pattern that travels along the bus and is detected by the senders.

6 The first sender to detect a collision sends a special signal that jams the network so that all nodes will know that the network is blocked. Transmissions from all nodes are halted, and each node waits a random length of time before trying to resend its message. The process repeats itself until one of the nodes sends its message without encountering another node's message.

Token-Ring Network

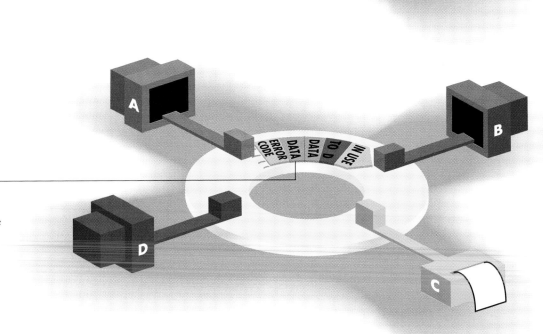

1 All nodes on a token-ring network are connected to the same circuit, which takes the form of a continuous loop. A *token*—which consists of a short all-clear message—circulates continuously along a loop and is read through a token-ring adapter card in each node as the token passes by.

2 A node wanting to send a message grabs the token as it passes by, changes the binary code in the token to say that it is in use, and attaches the node's message along with the address of the node for which the message is intended and the error-checking code. Only one message at a time can be circulated on the network.

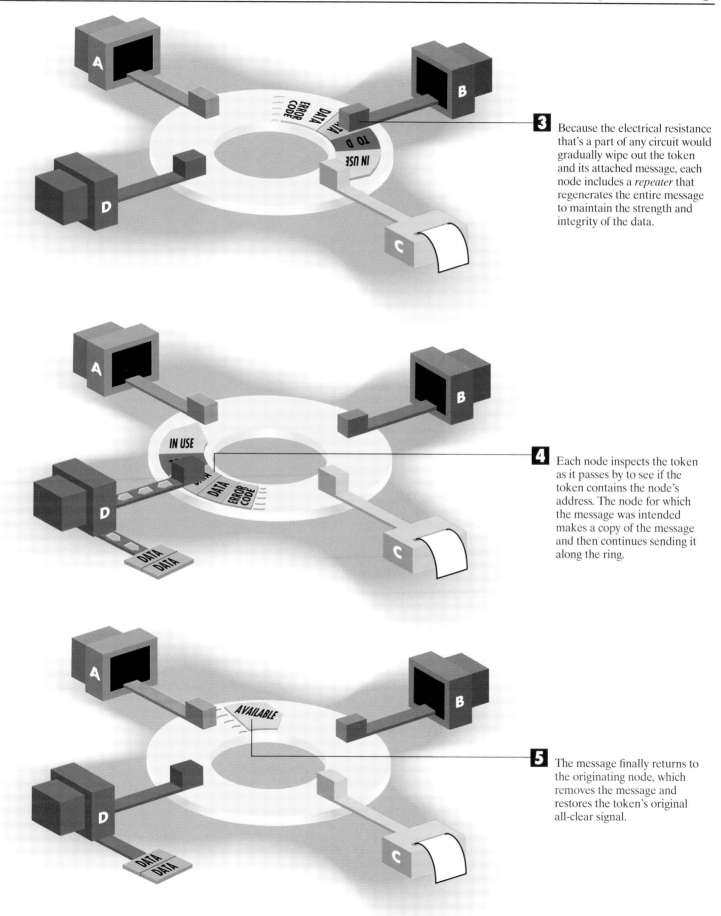

3 Because the electrical resistance that's a part of any circuit would gradually wipe out the token and its attached message, each node includes a *repeater* that regenerates the entire message to maintain the strength and integrity of the data.

4 Each node inspects the token as it passes by to see if the token contains the node's address. The node for which the message was intended makes a copy of the message and then continues sending it along the ring.

5 The message finally returns to the originating node, which removes the message and restores the token's original all-clear signal.

Star Network

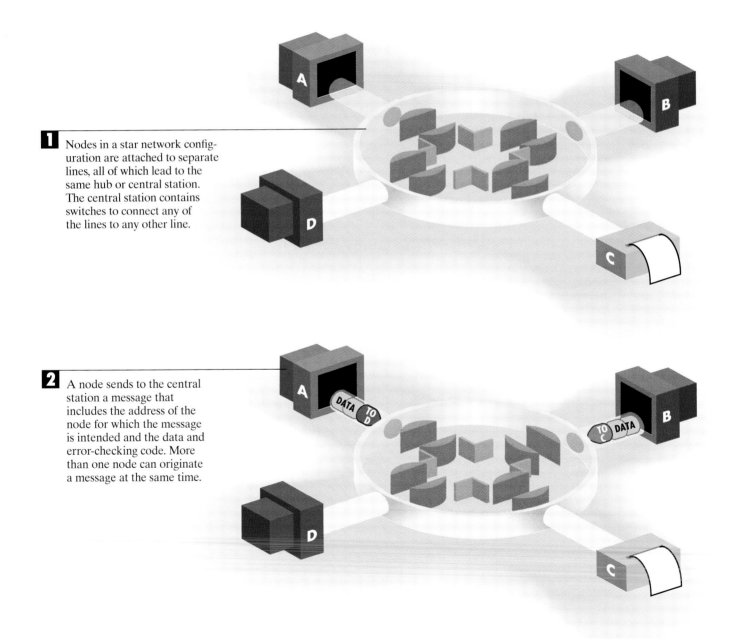

1 Nodes in a star network configuration are attached to separate lines, all of which lead to the same hub or central station. The central station contains switches to connect any of the lines to any other line.

2 A node sends to the central station a message that includes the address of the node for which the message is intended and the data and error-checking code. More than one node can originate a message at the same time.

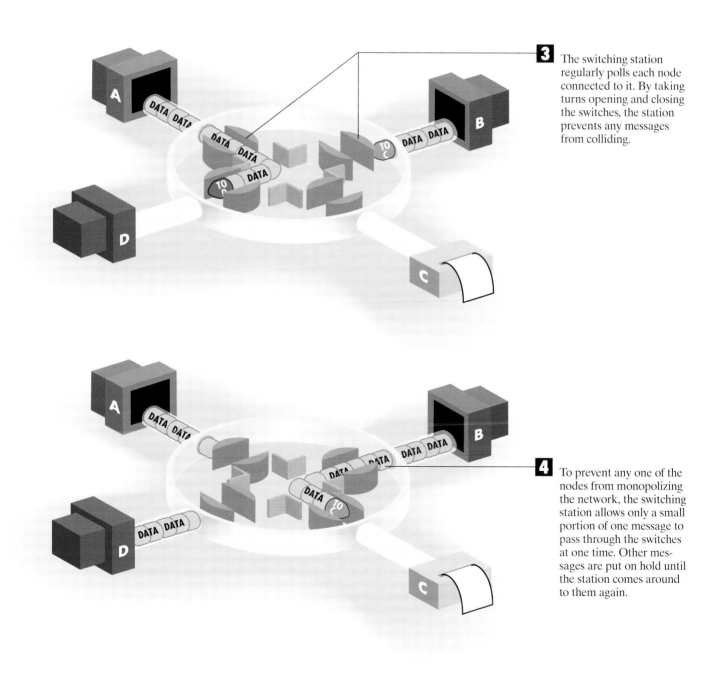

3 The switching station regularly polls each node connected to it. By taking turns opening and closing the switches, the station prevents any messages from colliding.

4 To prevent any one of the nodes from monopolizing the network, the switching station allows only a small portion of one message to pass through the switches at one time. Other messages are put on hold until the station comes around to them again.

CHAPTER

27

How Network Communications Work

SENDING MESSAGES ON a network is not simply a process of transmitting the bits that stand for alphanumeric characters. Network communications can involve DOS personal computers, Macintosh PCs, mainframes, and minicomputers, all of which have their own standards for encoding data and communicating. Add to that the fact that applications on each platform have their own standards for communications, and you'll see that sending and receiving even the simplest data becomes a gargantuan undertaking.

To make sure that data from one node on a computer reaches the other node or server for which it's intended—and that it arrives intact and uncorrupted—requires a system that's understood by all the components of a network. One such system is the Open Systems Interconnection (OSI) model, upon which many PC networks are based.

The seven-layer OSI model is not a specific collection of hardware and software, but rather it's a scheme that can be implemented in various ways as long as the implementation follows the OSI pattern. That pattern is based on layers: Each component of the network is said to exist on a specific layer of the system, and each component can communicate directly only with the layer directly above it and directly below it. Each layer provides services to the layer above it and can invoke the services of the layer below it.

Network Communications

1 **The application layer** is the only part of the communications process that a user sees, and even then, the user doesn't see most of the work that the application does to prepare a message for sending over a network. The layer converts a message's data from human-readable form into bits and attaches a header identifying the sending and receiving computers.

2 **The presentation layer** ensures that the message is transmitted in a language that the receiving computer can interpret (often ASCII). This layer translates the language, if necessary, and then compresses and perhaps encrypts the data. It adds another header specifying the language as well as the compression and encryption schemes.

3 **The session layer** opens communications and has the job of keeping straight the communications among all nodes on the network. It sets boundaries (called *bracketing*) for the beginning and end of the message, and establishes whether the message will be sent *half-duplex*, with each computer taking turns sending and receiving, or *full duplex*, with both computers sending and receiving at the same time. The details of these decisions are placed into a session header.

4 **The transport layer** protects the data being sent. It subdivides the data into segments, creates *checksum* tests—mathematical sums based on the contents of data—that can be used later to determine if the data was scrambled. It can also make backup copies of the data. The transport header identifies each segment's checksum and its position in the message.

5 **The network layer** selects a route for the message. It forms data into packets, counts them, and adds a header containing the sequence of packets and the address of the receiving computer.

6 **The data-link layer** supervises the transmission. It confirms the checksum, then addresses and duplicates the packets. This layer keeps a copy of each packet until it receives confirmation from the next point along the route that the packet has arrived undamaged.

7 **The physical layer** encodes the packets into the medium that will carry them—such as an analog signal, if the message is going across a telephone line—and sends the packets along that medium.

Header ___

Header ___

Header ___

Header ___

Header ___

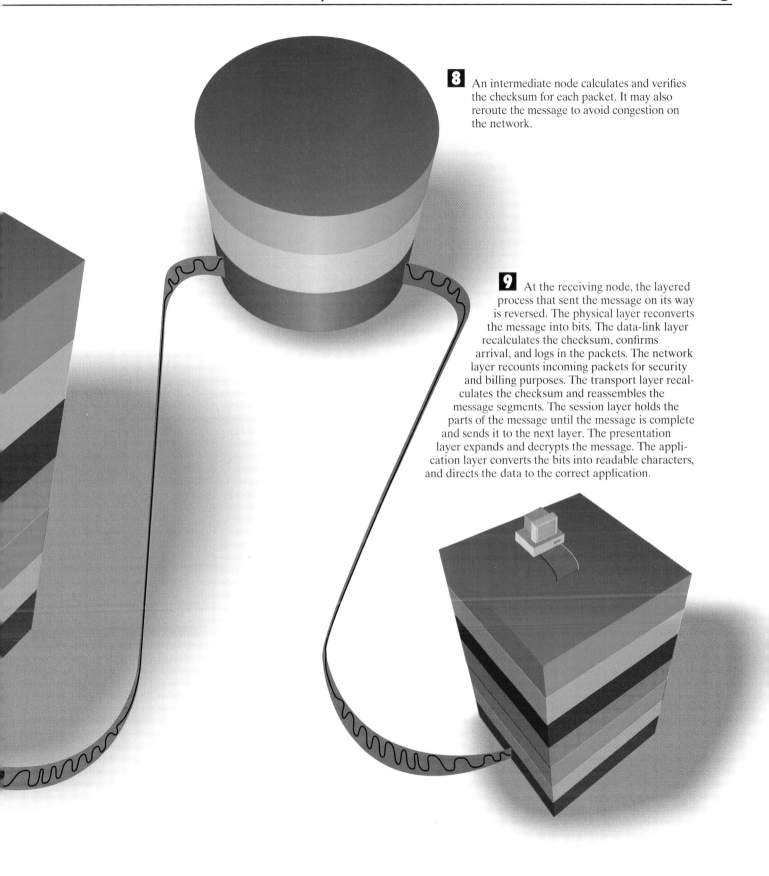

8 An intermediate node calculates and verifies the checksum for each packet. It may also reroute the message to avoid congestion on the network.

9 At the receiving node, the layered process that sent the message on its way is reversed. The physical layer reconverts the message into bits. The data-link layer recalculates the checksum, confirms arrival, and logs in the packets. The network layer recounts incoming packets for security and billing purposes. The transport layer recalculates the checksum and reassembles the message segments. The session layer holds the parts of the message until the message is complete and sends it to the next layer. The presentation layer expands and decrypts the message. The application layer converts the bits into readable characters, and directs the data to the correct application.

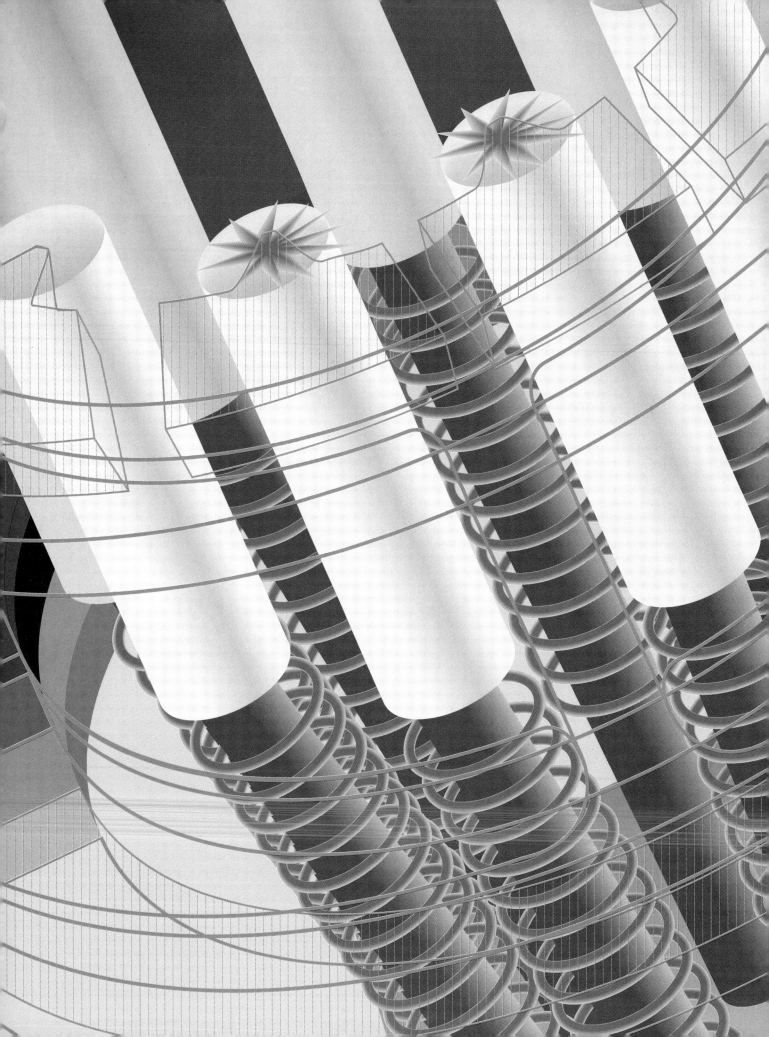

PRINTERS 6

CONTENTS

OVERVIEW

N THE EARLY days of personal computers, someone came up with the idea that all this computerized data would lead to the "paperless office." We're more than a decade into the personal computer revolution and more trees than ever are giving their lives to produce hard copies of everything from company budgets complete with full-color graphs to homemade greeting cards. Not only are we creating more printouts than ever before, but computer printing has turned into a fine art. The very essence of a whole new category of software—desktop publishing—is the accomplishment of better and better printed pages.

Whoever made that erroneous prediction about a paperless office missed an important fact. That person was probably thinking about how offices used paper in the age of the typewriter. Then there wasn't much you could put on paper except black letters and numbers—most often in an efficient but drab typeface called Courier. If all those ugly memos and letters had been replaced by electronic mail, the world would not have suffered a great loss. But what happened is that most people didn't predict back then that software and printing technology would make possible the fast, easy hard-copy versions of reports, newsletters, graphs, and, yes, memos and letters that even IBM's best Selectric could never come close to producing.

Speed and ease were the first improvements in printing. Where a simple typo on a typewriter might just be whited out or hand-corrected with a pen, today—because of the speed of printers—it's easier just to correct a mistake on screen and print a fresh, flawless copy.

Graphics were the next big advance. The day of the all-text document ended with the first software that could print even the crudest line graph on a dot-matrix printer. Now anything that's visual, from line art to halftone photograph, can be printed on a standard office printer.

Today, color is the current frontier being conquered with office printers. The quality and speed of color printers is increasing as their cost is decreasing. Because black-and-white printers are getting even faster and cheaper, we aren't likely to see color printers entirely replace monochrome printers, but they will start showing up in more offices on networks where they can be shared.

And, paper hasn't disappeared from the office. Instead, it's taken on a whole new importance. And the lowly printer that used to turn out crude approximations of characters is now one of the most important components of a computer system.

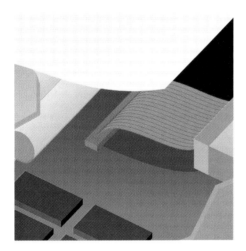

How Bitmapped and Outline Fonts Work

ALL PRINTERS, WHETHER dot-matrix, ink-jet, laser, or thermal, accomplish essentially the same task: They create a pattern of dots on a sheet of paper. The dots may be sized differently or composed of different inks transferred to the paper by different means, but all of the images for text and graphics are made up of dots. The smaller the dots, the more attractive the end result will be.

Regardless of how the dots are created on paper, there has to be a common scheme for determining where to place the dots; the most common schemes are bitmaps and outline fonts. Bitmapped fonts come in predefined sizes and weights. Outline fonts can be scaled and given special attributes on the fly. Each has its advantages and disadvantages, depending on what type of output you want.

Bitmapped images are generally limited to text and are a fast way to produce a printed page that uses only a few type fonts. If the hard copy is to include a graphic image in addition to bitmapped text, then, to create the graphic, your software must be able to send the printer instructions that it will understand.

Outline fonts are used with a page description language that treats everything on a page—even text—as a graphic. The text and graphics used by the software are converted to a series of commands that the printer's page description language uses to determine where each dot is to be placed on a page. Page description languages generally are slower at producing hard copy, but they are more versatile at producing different sizes of type with different attributes or special effects, and they create more attractive results.

Bitmapped Fonts

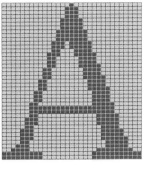
36 pt. medium

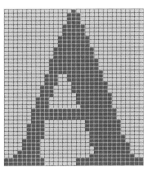
36 pt. bold

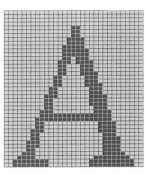
30 pt. medium

1 Bit-mapped fonts are typefaces of a certain size and with specific attributes or characteristics, such as boldface or italic. The bitmap is a record of the pattern of dots needed to create a specific character in a certain size and with a certain attribute. The bitmaps for a 36-point Times Roman medium capital *A*, for a 36-point Times Roman boldface capital *A*, and for a 30-point Times Roman medium capital *A* are all different and specific.

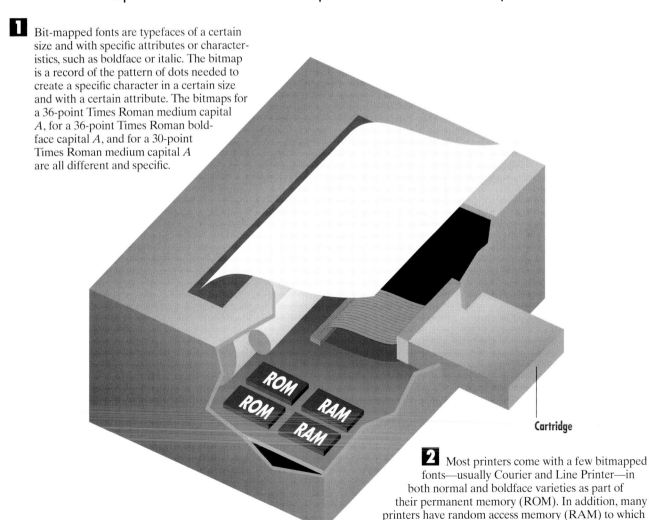

Cartridge

2 Most printers come with a few bitmapped fonts—usually Courier and Line Printer—in both normal and boldface varieties as part of their permanent memory (ROM). In addition, many printers have random access memory (RAM) to which your computer can send bitmaps for other fonts. You can also add additional bitmapped fonts in the form of plug-in cartridges used by many laser printers.

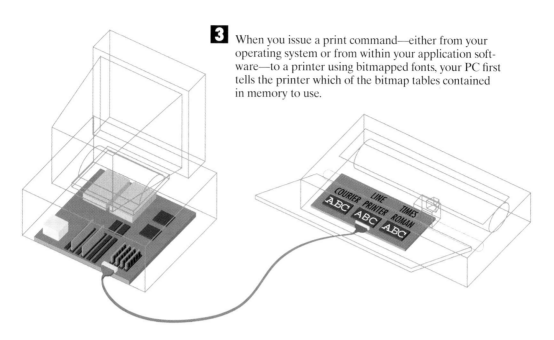

3 When you issue a print command—either from your operating system or from within your application software—to a printer using bitmapped fonts, your PC first tells the printer which of the bitmap tables contained in memory to use.

4 Then for each letter, punctuation mark, or paper movement—such as a tab or carriage return—that the software wants the printer to create, the PC sends an ASCII code. ASCII codes consist of hexadecimal numbers that are matched against the table of bitmaps. (Hexadecimal numbers have a base of 16—1, 2, 3, 4, 5, 6, 7, 8, 9, 0, A, B, C, D, E, F—instead of the base 10 used by decimal numbers.) If, for example, the hexadecimal number 41 (65 decimal) is sent to the printer, the printer's processor looks up 41h in its table and finds that it corresponds to a pattern of dots that creates an uppercase *A* in whatever typeface, type size, and attribute is in the active table.

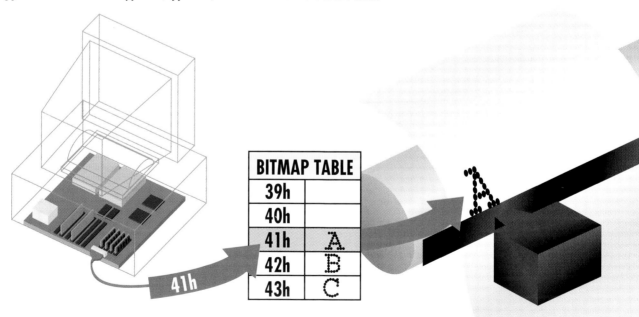

BITMAP TABLE	
39h	
40h	
41h	A
42h	B
43h	C

5 The printer uses that bitmap to determine which instructions to send to its other components to reproduce the bitmap's pattern on paper. Each character, one after the other, is sent to the printer.

Outline Fonts

36pt

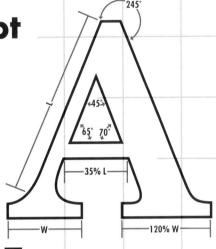

24pt

1 Outline fonts, unlike bitmapped fonts, are not limited to specific sizes and attributes of a typeface. Instead, they consist of mathematical descriptions of each character and punctuation mark in a typeface. They are called outline fonts because the outline of a Times Roman 36-point capital *A* is the same as that of a 24-point Times Roman capital *A*.

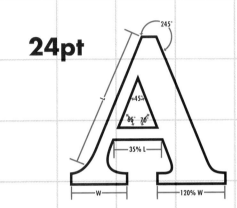

2 Some printers come with a page description language, most commonly PostScript or Hewlett-Packard Printer Command Language, in *firmware*—a computer program contained on a microchip. The language can translate outline font commands from your PC's software into the instructions the printer needs to control where it places dots on a sheet of paper. For printers that don't have a built-in page description language, PC software can translate the printer language commands into the instructions the printer needs.

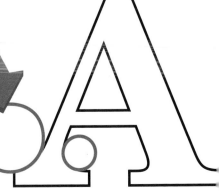

3 When you issue a print command from your application software to a printer using outline fonts, your application sends a series of commands the page description language interprets through a set of algorithms, or mathematical formulas. The algorithms describe the lines and arcs that make up the characters in a typeface. The algorithms for some typefaces include *hints*, special alterations to the outlines if the type is to be either extremely big or extremely small.

4 The commands insert variables into the formulas to change the size or attributes of the outline font. The results are commands to the printer that say, in effect, "Create a horizontal line 3 points wide, which begins 60 points from the bottom and 20 points to the right." The page description language turns on all the bits that fall inside the outline of the letter—unless the font includes some special shading effect within the outline.

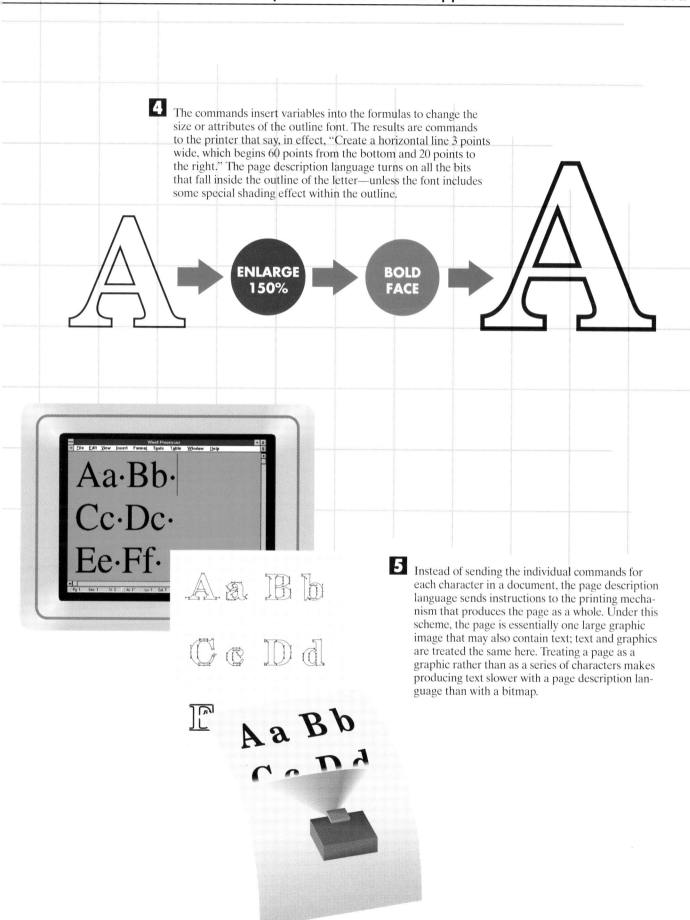

ENLARGE
150%

BOLD
FACE

5 Instead of sending the individual commands for each character in a document, the page description language sends instructions to the printing mechanism that produces the page as a whole. Under this scheme, the page is essentially one large graphic image that may also contain text; text and graphics are treated the same here. Treating a page as a graphic rather than as a series of characters makes producing text slower with a page description language than with a bitmap.

CHAPTER 29

How a Dot-Matrix Printer Works

ALTHOUGH LASER PRINTERS are faster and produce more attractive documents, the mechanical dot-matrix printer continues to be a mainstay of many computer systems. Laser printers often cost more than $1,000; a reliable dot-matrix printer costs only a few hundred. Laser printers require replacing a toner cartridge that costs nearly as much as a low-end dot-matrix printer; all a dot-matrix printer needs in the way of supplies is a new ribbon, now and then, which you can buy for pocket change.

Dot-matrix printers are a necessity for tasks that require printing on multilayer forms, something the nonimpact laser printer can't do at all. And today's 24-pin dot-matrix printers increase both the printer's speed and the quality of the type.

Manufacturers continue to introduce newer, faster, more intelligent—even less noisy—dot-matrix printers to receptive users. Chances are good that dot-matrix impact printers will stay with us for years to come.

Although some dot-matrix printers can interpret commands from PostScript or some other page description language, most impact printers are designed to work with bitmapped type controlled by ASCII codes sent to the printer from a PC. (See "How Bitmapped and Outline Fonts Work" for details on page description languages and bitmapped type.)

Dot-Matrix Printer

1 Your PC sends a series of ASCII codes that represent characters, punctuation marks, and printer movements such as tabs, carriage returns, and form feeds, which control the position of the print head in relation to the paper.

2 The ASCII codes are stored in a buffer, which is a special section of the printer's random access memory (RAM). Because it usually takes longer for a dot-matrix printer to print characters than it takes a PC and software to send those characters to the printer, the buffer helps free up the PC to perform other functions during printing. The internal buffer of a dot-matrix printer generally has only a 7k to 8k capacity. When the buffer gets full, the printer sends an XOFF control code to the computer to tell it to suspend its stream of data. When the buffer frees up space by sending some of the characters to its processor, the printer sends an XON code to the PC, which resumes sending data.

3 Among those codes are commands that tell the printer to use a certain font's bitmap table, which is contained in the printer's read-only memory chips. That table tells the printer the pattern of dots that it should use to create the characters represented by the ASCII codes.

4 The printer's processor takes the information provided by the bitmap table for an entire line of type and calculates the most efficient path for the print head to travel. (Some lines may actually be printed from right to left.) The processor sends the signals that fire the pins in the print head, and it also controls the movements of the print head and platen.

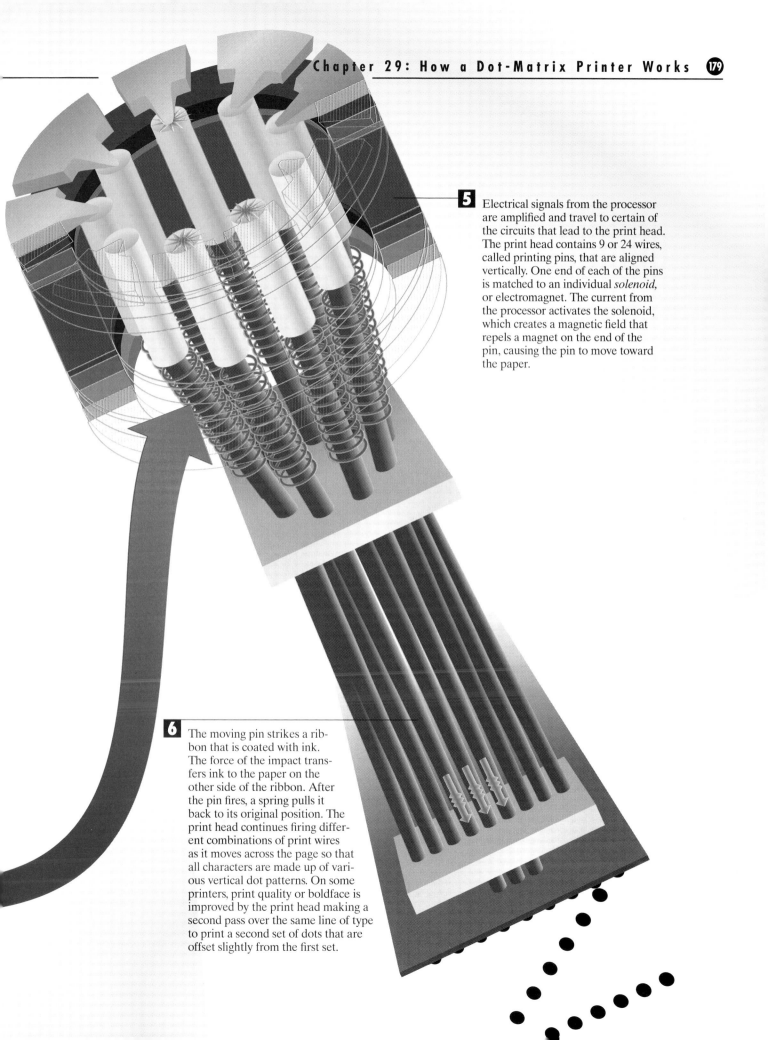

5 Electrical signals from the processor are amplified and travel to certain of the circuits that lead to the print head. The print head contains 9 or 24 wires, called printing pins, that are aligned vertically. One end of each of the pins is matched to an individual *solenoid*, or electromagnet. The current from the processor activates the solenoid, which creates a magnetic field that repels a magnet on the end of the pin, causing the pin to move toward the paper.

6 The moving pin strikes a ribbon that is coated with ink. The force of the impact transfers ink to the paper on the other side of the ribbon. After the pin fires, a spring pulls it back to its original position. The print head continues firing different combinations of print wires as it moves across the page so that all characters are made up of various vertical dot patterns. On some printers, print quality or boldface is improved by the print head making a second pass over the same line of type to print a second set of dots that are offset slightly from the first set.

How a Laser Printer Works

EVERY TIME YOU send a page to your laser printer, you're setting in motion a complex series of steps as efficiently organized as a factory and as precisely choreographed as a ballet.

At the heart of the printer is the *print engine*—the mechanism that transfers a black powder to the page—which is a device that owes its ancestry to the photocopier. Its parts represent the highest state of printing technology, including laser imaging, precise paper movement, and microprocessor control of all its actions.

To create the nearly typeset-quality output that is characteristic of a laser printer, the printer must control five different operations at the same time: (1) It must interpret the signals coming from a computer, (2) translate those signals into instructions that control the movement of a laser beam, (3) control the movement of the paper, (4) sensitize the paper so that it will accept the black toner that makes up the image, and (5) fuse that image to the paper.

The result is no-compromise printing. Not only does the laser printer produce hard copy faster than does the dot-matrix printer, but the laser-printed pages are more sharply detailed than those of the dot-matrix. The laser printer, for the foreseeable future, represents the standard for high-end computerized printing.

Laser Printer

2 The instructions from the printer's processor rapidly turn on and off a beam of light from a laser.

1 Your PC's operating system or software sends signals to the laser printer to determine where each dot of printing toner is to be placed on the paper. The signals are one of two types—either a simple ASCII code or a page description language command. (See "How Bitmapped and Outline Fonts Work.")

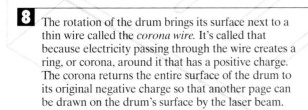

10 The paper train pushes the paper out of the printer, usually with the printed side down so that pages end up in the output tray in the correct order.

9 Another set of rollers pulls the paper through a part of the print engine called the *fusing system.* There pressure and heat bind the toner permanently to the paper by melting and pressing a wax that is part of the toner. The heat from the fusing system is what causes paper fresh from a laser printer to be warm.

8 The rotation of the drum brings its surface next to a thin wire called the *corona wire.* It's called that because electricity passing through the wire creates a ring, or corona, around it that has a positive charge. The corona returns the entire surface of the drum to its original negative charge so that another page can be drawn on the drum's surface by the laser beam.

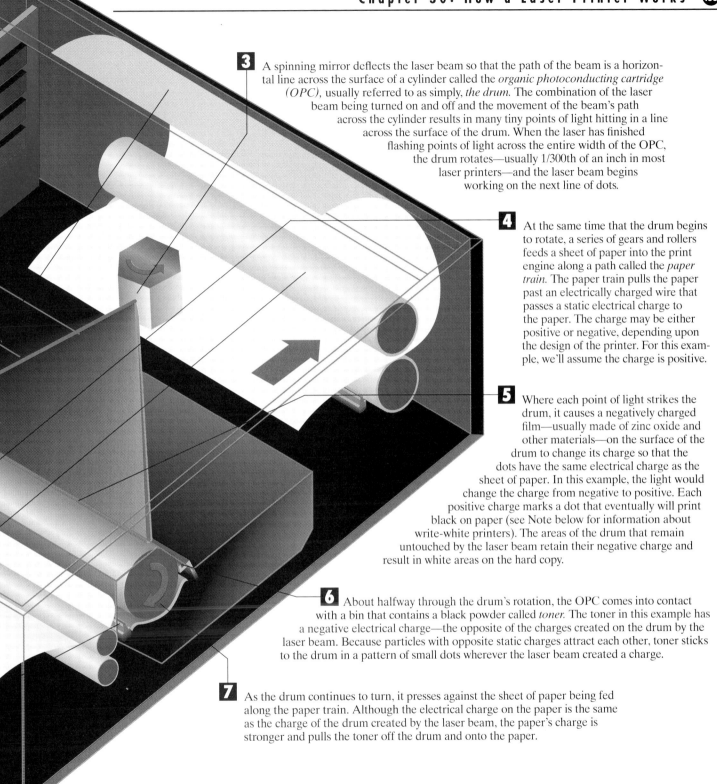

3 A spinning mirror deflects the laser beam so that the path of the beam is a horizontal line across the surface of a cylinder called the *organic photoconducting cartridge (OPC)*, usually referred to as simply, *the drum.* The combination of the laser beam being turned on and off and the movement of the beam's path across the cylinder results in many tiny points of light hitting in a line across the surface of the drum. When the laser has finished flashing points of light across the entire width of the OPC, the drum rotates—usually 1/300th of an inch in most laser printers—and the laser beam begins working on the next line of dots.

4 At the same time that the drum begins to rotate, a series of gears and rollers feeds a sheet of paper into the print engine along a path called the *paper train.* The paper train pulls the paper past an electrically charged wire that passes a static electrical charge to the paper. The charge may be either positive or negative, depending upon the design of the printer. For this example, we'll assume the charge is positive.

5 Where each point of light strikes the drum, it causes a negatively charged film—usually made of zinc oxide and other materials—on the surface of the drum to change its charge so that the dots have the same electrical charge as the sheet of paper. In this example, the light would change the charge from negative to positive. Each positive charge marks a dot that eventually will print black on paper (see Note below for information about write-white printers). The areas of the drum that remain untouched by the laser beam retain their negative charge and result in white areas on the hard copy.

6 About halfway through the drum's rotation, the OPC comes into contact with a bin that contains a black powder called *toner.* The toner in this example has a negative electrical charge—the opposite of the charges created on the drum by the laser beam. Because particles with opposite static charges attract each other, toner sticks to the drum in a pattern of small dots wherever the laser beam created a charge.

7 As the drum continues to turn, it presses against the sheet of paper being fed along the paper train. Although the electrical charge on the paper is the same as the charge of the drum created by the laser beam, the paper's charge is stronger and pulls the toner off the drum and onto the paper.

NOTE In the description above, the electrical charges in all instances can be reversed and the result would be the same. The method described here is true of most printers that use the Canon print engine, such as Hewlett-Packard models, which are the standard among laser printers. This approach is called *write-black* because every dot etched on the printer drum by the laser beam marks a place that will be black on the printout. However, there is an alternative way that a laser printer can work and that way produces noticeably different results. The other method, used by Ricoh print engines, is called *write-white* because everywhere the laser beam strikes, it creates a charge the same as that of the toner—the toner is attracted to the areas not affected by the beam of light. Write-white printers generally produce darker black areas, and write-black printers generally produce finer details.

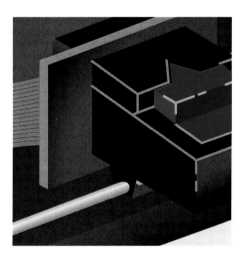

How an Ink-Jet Printer Works

NK-JET PRINTERS OCCUPY a niche between dot-matrix impact printers and laser printers. These small printers that fit on nearly any desk share the fine resolution of laser printers. Only with the closest inspection are you likely to detect the difference between laser and ink-jet output.

And like laser devices, ink-jets spare you the insect whine and chatter that accompany impact printers. All you hear is a slight whisper followed by a low thunk as a page is ejected.

For all their similarity to laser printers, however, ink-jets really more resemble dot-matrix printers. They both have print heads that travel across the width of a page, depositing an entire line of text with each pass. (See "How a Dot-Matrix Printer Works" for more details on how printing commands are interpreted by any printer that uses a matrix print head.) This mechanical movement puts ink-jet printers in the same speed class as impact printers, but ink-jets deposit ink in much smaller dots than do impact printers. The price of ink-jets is usually close to that of dot-matrix printers. They are the perfect compromise of cost, speed, and quality.

The biggest difference between ink-jet printers and both of its cousins is the ink-jet's print head. Using a technology so unusual that you wonder how anyone ever thought of it, an ink-jet printer spits little drops of ink onto paper. It's a technology that works much better than you would imagine and also lends itself readily to inexpensive color printing.

Ink-Jet Printer

1 An ink-filled print cartridge attached to the ink-jet's print head moves sideways across the width of a sheet of paper that is fed through the printer below the print head.

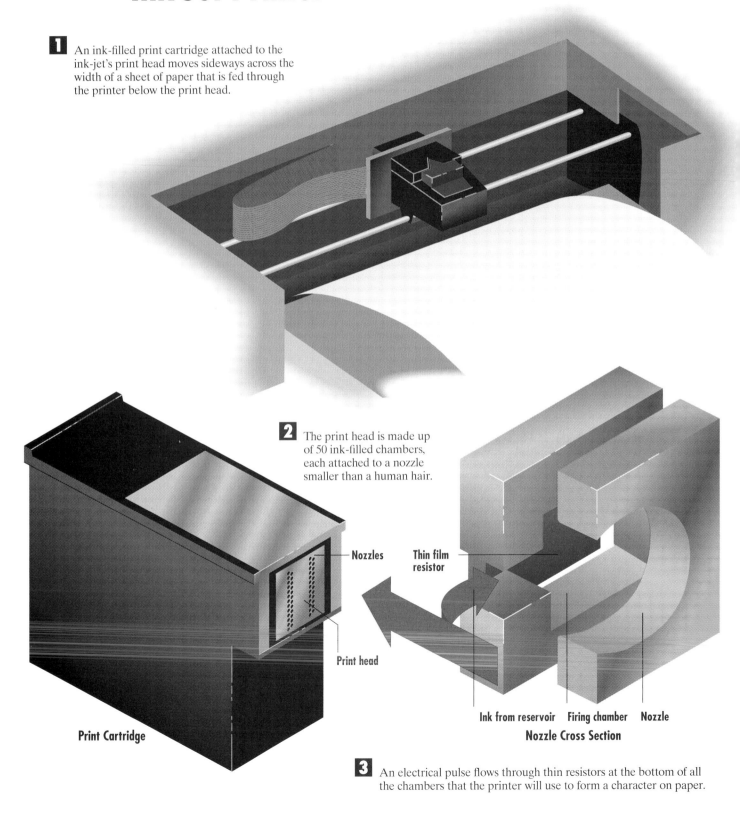

2 The print head is made up of 50 ink-filled chambers, each attached to a nozzle smaller than a human hair.

Nozzles

Thin film resistor

Print head

Ink from reservoir   Firing chamber   Nozzle

Nozzle Cross Section

Print Cartridge

3 An electrical pulse flows through thin resistors at the bottom of all the chambers that the printer will use to form a character on paper.

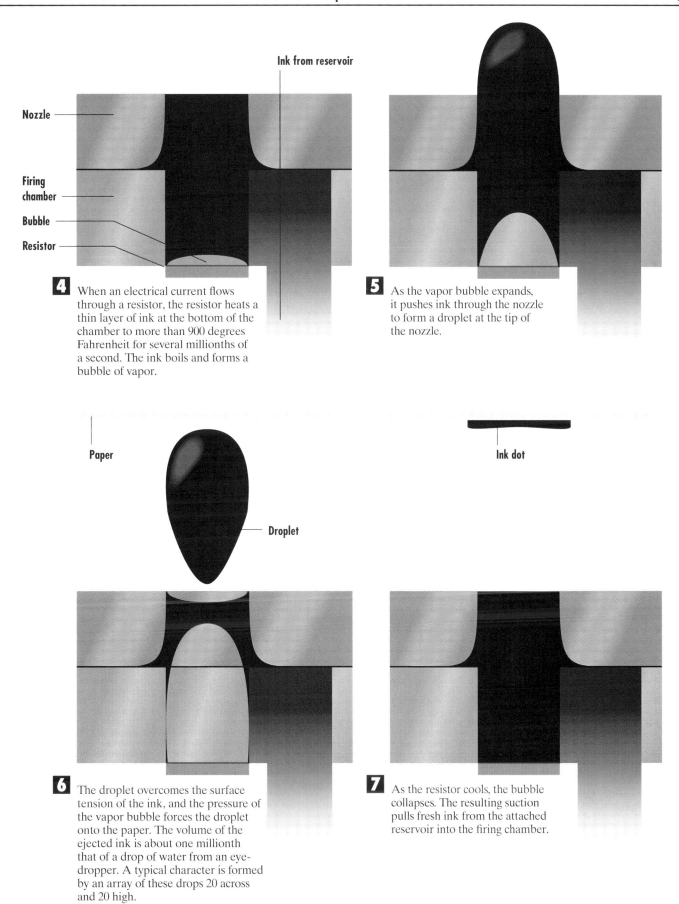

Ink from reservoir

Nozzle

Firing chamber

Bubble

Resistor

4 When an electrical current flows through a resistor, the resistor heats a thin layer of ink at the bottom of the chamber to more than 900 degrees Fahrenheit for several millionths of a second. The ink boils and forms a bubble of vapor.

5 As the vapor bubble expands, it pushes ink through the nozzle to form a droplet at the tip of the nozzle.

Paper

Droplet

Ink dot

6 The droplet overcomes the surface tension of the ink, and the pressure of the vapor bubble forces the droplet onto the paper. The volume of the ejected ink is about one millionth that of a drop of water from an eye-dropper. A typical character is formed by an array of these drops 20 across and 20 high.

7 As the resistor cools, the bubble collapses. The resulting suction pulls fresh ink from the attached reservoir into the firing chamber.

How a Color Thermal Printer Works

FAST, INEXPENSIVE COLOR printing is the holy grail of printer manufacturers. Although color printers are getting faster, smaller, and less expensive, the very nature of combining colors on the same sheet of paper automatically makes the process complicated.

Anytime you look at a color-printed page, you're actually looking at a complex arrangement of only four colors of ink—cyan (blue), magenta (red), yellow, and black. (Sometimes black is not included because a printer can create black—usually with not entirely satisfactory results—by combining equal portions of the other three colors.) If you look closely at a magnified section of a color-printed page, you'll see a pattern of colored dots.

Because each printed color is made up of at least three separate colors, each page must, in effect, be printed at least three times. To the time it takes to perform all these mechanical movements, add the processing time your software requires to figure out the correct mixtures of colors and generate the instructions to the printer, and the result is an invariably slow process.

Some of the earliest color printers were based on variations of the techniques used in traditional black printing. Dot-matrix impact printers use ribbons with three or four bands of colored ink. Ink-jet printers use three or four print heads, each with an accompanying cartridge of colored ink. The most recent development has been color laser printers, which run paper past separate toners for each color.

The most common professional color-printing device in use is the color thermal printer, shown here. The process provides vivid colors because the inks it uses don't bleed into each other or soak into specially coated paper. There have been other advances made in desktop color printing, but for now, color thermal printing is the standard method.

Color Thermal Printer

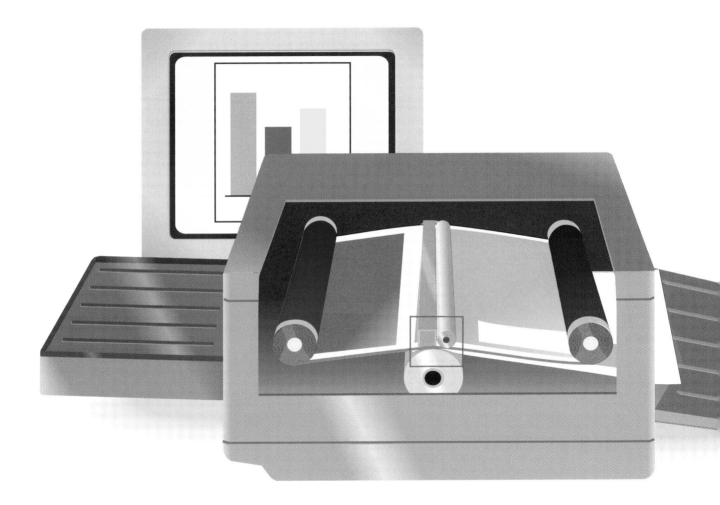

1 The color thermal printer feeds a sheet of specially coated paper from its bin into the print engine, where the paper is held on one side by a roller that presses the paper against a wide ribbon coated with colored inks mixed with wax or plastic. The ribbon contains a band of each of the composite printing colors—cyan, magenta, yellow and, if it's used, black. Each color band covers a large area—the width and length of the sheet of paper.

2 As the paper passes through the paper train, it first presses against the cyan band of the ribbon. One or more heating elements arranged in a row on the thermal print head on the other side of the ribbon are turned on and melt small dots of the cyan dye. The melted dots are pressed against the paper.

3 The paper continues moving through the paper train until it is partially ejected from the printer. As the paper peels away from the ribbon, the unmelted cyan ink remains on the ribbon and the melted dye sticks to the paper.

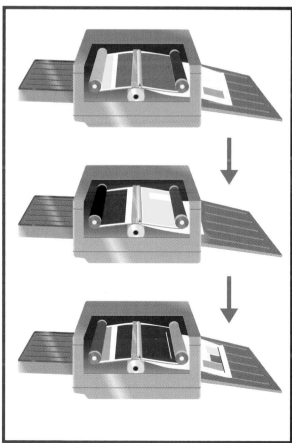

4 The color ribbon turns to expose the magenta band, and the paper is pulled back into the printer, where it presses against the magenta band of the ribbon and the thermal process is repeated. The process repeats itself for all of the colors used by the printer, and then the page is completely ejected.

Imagination.
Innovation. Insight.

The How It Works Series from Ziff-Davis Press

"... a magnificently seamless integration of text and graphics ..."

Larry Blasko, The Associated Press, reviewing *PC/Computing How Computers Work*

No other books bring computer technology to life like the *How It Works* series from Ziff-Davis Press. Lavish, full-color illustrations and lucid text from some of the world's top computer commentators make *How It Works* books an exciting way to explore the inner workings of PC technology.

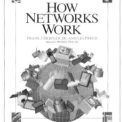

PC/Computing How Computers Work

A worldwide blockbuster that hit the general trade bestseller lists! *PC/Computing* magazine executive editor Ron White dismantles the PC and reveals what really makes it tick.

ISBN: 094-7 Price: $22.95

How Networks Work

Two of the most respected names in connectivity showcase the PC network, illustrating and explaining how each component does its magic and how they all fit together.

ISBN: 129-3 Price: $24.95

How Macs Work

A fun and fascinating voyage to the heart of the Macintosh! Two noted *MacUser* contributors cover the spectrum of Macintosh operations from startup to shutdown.

How Software Works

This dazzlingly illustrated volume from Ron White peeks inside the PC to show in full-color how software breathes life into the PC. Covers Windows™ and all major software categories.

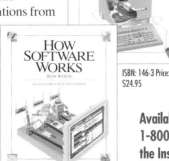

ISBN: 133-1 Price: $24.95

How to Use Your Computer

Conquer computerphobia and see how this intricate machine truly makes life easier. Dozens of full-color graphics showcase the components of the PC and explain how to interact with them.

All About Computers

This one-of-a-kind visual guide for kids features numerous full-color illustrations and photos on every page, combined with dozens of interactive projects that reinforce computer basics, making this an exciting way to learn all about the world of computers.

How To Use Word

Make Word 6.0 for Windows Work for You!

A uniquely visual approach puts the basics of Microsoft's latest Windows-based word processor right before the reader's eyes. Colorful examples invite them to begin producing a variety of documents, quickly and easily. Truly innovative!

ISBN: 184-6 Price: $17.95

How To Use Excel

Make Excel 5.0 for Windows Work for You!

Covering the latest version of Excel, this visually impressive resource guides beginners to spreadsheet fluency through a full-color graphical approach that makes powerful techniques seem plain as day. Hands-on "Try It" sections give new users a chance to sharpen newfound skills.

ISBN: 146-3 Price: $24.95

HOW TO USE YOUR COMPUTER
LISA BIOW
ISBN: 155-2 Price: $22.95

ALL ABOUT COMPUTERS
JEAN ATELSEK
ISBN: 166-8 Price: $15.95

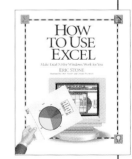
ISBN: 185-4 Price: $17.95

Available at all fine bookstores or by calling 1-800-688-0448, ext. 100. Call for more information on the Instructor's Supplement, including transparencies for each book in the *How It Works* Series.

ZIFF-DAVIS ZD PRESS

© 1993 Ziff-Davis Press

ATTENTION TEACHERS AND TRAINERS
Now You Can Teach From These Books!

ZD Press now offers instructors and trainers
the materials they need to use these books in their classes.

- An Instructor's Manual features flexible lessons designed for use in a 10- or 15-week course (30-45 course hours).

- Student exercises and tests on floppy disk provide you with an easy way to tailor and/or duplicate tests as you need them.

- A Transparency Package contains all the graphics from the book, each on a single, full-color transparency.

- Spanish edition of *PC/Computing How Computers Work* will be available.

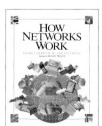

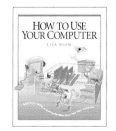
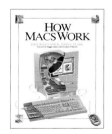

Ziff-Davis Press Survey of Readers

Please help us in our effort to produce the best books on personal computing.
For your assistance, we would be pleased to send you a FREE catalog
featuring the complete line of Ziff-Davis Press books.

1. How did you first learn about this book?

Recommended by a friend . . . . ☐ -1 (5)

Recommended by store personnel . . . .☐ -2

Saw in Ziff-Davis Press catalog . . . .☐ -3

Received advertisement in the mail . . . .☐ -4

Saw the book on bookshelf at store . . . .☐ -5

Read book review in: _____ ☐ -6

Saw an advertisement in: _____ ☐ -7

Other (Please specify): _____ ☐ -8

2. Which THREE of the following factors most influenced your decision to purchase this book? (Please check up to THREE.)

Front or back cover information on book . . .☐ -1 (6)

Logo of magazine affiliated with book . . . . . .☐ -2

Special approach to the content . . . .☐ -3

Completeness of content . . . .☐ -4

Author's reputation. . . . .☐ -5

Publisher's reputation . . . .☐ -6

Book cover design or layout . . . .☐ -7

Index or table of contents of book . . . .☐ -8

Price of book . . . .☐ -9

Special effects, graphics, illustrations . . . . . .☐ -0

Other (Please specify): _____ ☐ -x

3. How many computer books have you purchased in the last six months? _____   (7-10)

4. On a scale of 1 to 5, where 5 is excellent, 4 is above average, 3 is average, 2 is below average, and 1 is poor, please rate each of the following aspects of this book below. (Please circle your answer.)

Depth/completeness of coverage	5	4	3	2	1	(11)
Organization of material	5	4	3	2	1	(12)
Ease of finding topic	5	4	3	2	1	(13)
Special features/time saving tips	5	4	3	2	1	(14)
Appropriate level of writing	5	4	3	2	1	(15)
Usefulness of table of contents	5	4	3	2	1	(16)
Usefulness of index	5	4	3	2	1	(17)
Usefulness of accompanying disk	5	4	3	2	1	(18)
Usefulness of illustrations/graphics	5	4	3	2	1	(19)
Cover design and attractiveness	5	4	3	2	1	(20)
Overall design and layout of book	5	4	3	2	1	(21)
Overall satisfaction with book	5	4	3	2	1	(22)

5. Which of the following computer publications do you read regularly; that is, 3 out of 4 issues?

Byte . . . .☐ -1 (23)

Computer Shopper . . . .☐ -2

Corporate Computing . . . . ☐ -3

Dr. Dobb's Journal . . . .☐ -4

LAN Magazine . . . .☐ -5

MacWEEK . . . .☐ -6

MacUser . . . .☐ -7

PC Computing . . . .☐ -8

PC Magazine . . . .☐ -9

PC WEEK . . . .☐ -0

Windows Sources . . . .☐ -x

Other (Please specify): _____ ☐ -y

Please turn page.

Cut Here

Cut Here

PLEASE TAPE HERE ONLY—DO NOT STAPLE

6. What is your level of experience with personal computers? With the subject of this book?

	With PCs		With subject of book	
Beginner	☐	-1 (24)	☐	-1 (25)
Intermediate	☐	-2	☐	-2
Advanced	☐	-3	☐	-3

7. Which of the following best describes your job title?

Officer (CEO/President/VP/owner)	☐	-1 (26)
Director/head	☐	-2
Manager/supervisor	☐	-3
Administration/staff	☐	-4
Teacher/educator/trainer	☐	-5
Lawyer/doctor/medical professional	☐	-6
Engineer/technician	☐	-7
Consultant	☐	-8
Not employed/student/retired	☐	-9
Other (Please specify): ______________	☐	-0

8. What is your age?

Under 20	☐	-1 (27)
21-29	☐	-2
30-39	☐	-3
40-49	☐	-4
50-59	☐	-5
60 or over	☐	-6

9. Are you:

Male	☐	-1 (28)
Female	☐	-2

Thank you for your assistance with this important information! Please write your address below to receive our free catalog.

Name: ______________________________

Address: ______________________________

City/State/Zip: ______________________________

Fold here to mail.

2508-13-08

____

____

____

NO POSTAGE NECESSARY IF MAILED IN THE UNITED STATES

BUSINESS REPLY MAIL

FIRST CLASS MAIL PERMIT NO. 1612 OAKLAND, CA

POSTAGE WILL BE PAID BY ADDRESSEE

Ziff-Davis Press
5903 Christie Avenue
Emeryville, CA 94608-1925
Attn: Marketing